From Rock Singer To Hymns Ancient & Modern

Steve Flashman

Copyright © 2024 Steve Flashman
All rights reserved.
ISBN: 9798329418385

DEDICATION

To the wonderful people at Holy Cross & St Mary, Quainton and All Saints, Oving in Buckinghamshire, England and my colleagues in the Schorne Team of churches, for putting up with my rock 'n roll mentality, my 'creative' way of doing things and for always turning a blind eye when I forget the liturgical colours!

CONTENTS

1	Setting the Scene	1
2	100 Concerts a Year	4
3	What Makes Your Heart Beat Faster	7
4	The Joke About The Horse And Descartes	10
5	Thank God for Recycled Furniture	13
6	The Devil in a Boot	15
7	The Little Yellow Ducks	17
8	700 Years with God at Work	20
9	To Chasuble or not to Chasuble?	23
10	Like a Rock 'n Roll Singer!	26
11	Someone's Trying to Kill Me!	28
12	He Doesn't Do God, Church or Vicars!	31
13	Smashing the Myth	34
14	Matt Redman versus Ancient & Modern	38
15	What! The Church Runs a Beer Festival!	41
16	Shall I Bless the Chicken or Say Grace?	44
17	The Vicar Got the Turkey!	47
18	Five Services in One Day	50
19	Show 'em Your Cross!	54
20	You'll Never Get Them Singing 'Sha la la''	56

ACKNOWLEDGMENTS

My journey into the Anglican Church was aided and abetted by some wonderful people who encouraged, motivated, equipped and challenged me to make a difference for God.

My thanks to Rt Revd Donald Mtetemela, former Archbishop of Tanzania, Bishop John Gladwin, Bishop Martin Warner, Bishop Richard Jackson and the wonderful Revd Frank Goodwin, who enabled me to begin my journey into faith.

But most of all, my adorable wife Sarah, who literally saved my life on at least two occasions and has been right there at my side through thick and thin – and she always knows what the liturgical colours should be!

1 SETTING THE SCENE

I was 67 when we got the call to move to Oxford.

I am supposed to be slowing down, but I'm speeding up!

Many of my colleagues and friends who have been in church ministry are now retired and enjoying life in their mortgage free retirement property by the sea, enjoying country walks with the wife and the dog, cooking great food from the Jamie Oliver "how to cook wholesome and nourishing food in 10 minutes" recipe book, and doing the occasional guest preaching slot, picking their best sermons and favourite illustrations without all the demands of church leadership.

But not me.

There's something in me that always wants to take the toughest route, the most difficult journey, the more challenging adventure!

I'm not saying that this is an attribute, it's extremely annoying at times. Why me?

As they used to say in the old days, "Steve, you're making a rod for your own back!"

And now, on top of all that, I've landed my toughest assignment yet! Taking on two parish churches in rural Buckinghamshire and becoming a traditional vicar - right out of my comfort zone!

What will my children think?

They already know I'm a little crazy, but this assignment is in a different league. This is dad stepping into unknown territory. After all these years of "radicalness", he's finally flipped.

Will they think I have lost my marbles?

Have I finally entered into the alien zone of planet Zorg? I know what they're are thinking:

"These are the voyages of the Starship Enterprise. Its five year mission: to explore strange new worlds. To seek out new life and new civilisations. To go where no man has gone before!"

OK. I know I'm being over dramatic! But that's how it felt at the time.

These reflections contain an account of my personal journey during the first three years as Team Vicar with charge of two delightful rural churches, Holy Cross & St Mary, Quainton and All Saints, Oving.

We often fall into the trap of approaching life with pre-conceived ideas and mis-conceptions about people and situations that we've never really encountered. And all this is often driven by the media.

The only encounter I ever really had with rural church was watching the Vicar of Dibley on TV. I'm not naive enough to believe that's the way it really is, but you can understand why I was worried - and intrigued.

The fact is that the people I have come to know and love in these beautiful villages are nothing like the people of Dibley!

I learn from them in so many ways, and have come to appreciate God working in the most unlikely places and through people who give so much to the community.

Stay with me and I'll share with you many of the things I have discovered - mistakes made, lessons learned, and victories won!

Along the way I discover some important truths about myself and how to be effective as a priest in rural ministry. I discover that what I thought were my strengths, are actually weaknesses in this new assignment.

I learn lessons as my preconceived ideas about the traditional Anglican church are shot out of the water. I am educated into the value of real community and take a dip into the waters of choral Evensong.

Peoples' names have been changed to protect the innocent (and the guilty!) - you know who you are!

Let's get started.

2 100 CONCERTS A YEAR

I released my first album in 1978 on the Kingsway Music label and then more followed, releasing a new album every two to four years until I reached a grand total of ten.

During the years that I worked as a professional musician, I travelled all around the UK, then the Nederlands, then out to Canada. And from there India, Sri Lanka, the USA and all over Europe.

Ever since my teenage years, I've been passionate about connecting my Christian faith with people of all ages through contemporary music - not so much in churches, but in places where people meet.

So I performed my style of contemporary rock music in schools, universities, pubs, bars, clubs and theatres with the occasional skirmish into larger venues such as the Royal Albert Hall, Wembley Arena, the Marquee Club in Soho, Main Stage Greenbelt, Spring Harvest, Royal Week and various other music festivals.

I found myself singing to audiences ranging from less than a hundred to several thousand.

Numerous appearances on television and radio followed including the Rock Gospel Show on BBC, my own talk show on London's LBC Radio, the Breakfast Show on County Sound Radio, Guildford, where I was also Religious Affairs Producer and clocking up over 100 appearances on ITV co-presenting a religious current affairs programme called "Company."

I was even short listed to present Songs of Praise on the BBC but was pipped at the post by someone else - who still presents from time to time!

Several of my contemporaries chose to break into the commercial music business and some had minor success, but I always felt my calling was to create messages through music that would be accessible in the more specialised mission field of schools, clubs, bars, prisons and universities.

Over the 20 years or so that I was "on the road" I performed to tens of thousands of young people all over the world often performing in more than one hundred concerts a year.

Schools work has become known as 'the forgotten mission field'.

A typical "schools mission" would involve taking lessons on anything from current affairs to sex education. Obviously not "preaching" at the kids, but taking an educational approach, the doors were flung open in hundreds of schools around the UK and Europe.

After a typical week long mission we would organise a concert performance, inviting people to this main event to hear my Christian story and how the Good News of Jesus can transform our lives and our world. We saw thousands of young people giving their lives to Christ at these events.

It's one of the great joys of my life when I receive emails

and messages from people who made that commitment all those years ago and are still moving forward in their Christian faith.

I'd like to say a big thank you to those who travelled with me during those years, helping with PA systems, lighting rigs and media presentations including Richard Moyes, James Loring, Kevin (Boo Boo) Brown and Richard Baker. We drove tens of thousands of miles in our old Long Wheel Base Ford Transit van.

God bless 'em!

So how did I end up going from all of that, to all of this?

Stay tuned!

3 WHAT MAKES YOUR HEART BEAT FASTER?

Sarah and I had been co-leading a church in Chichester for ten years.

Together with the leaders of the church we caught a vision to re-open a decommissioned NHS Chapel on the Graylingwell Hospital site next to the University.

A developer bought the site with a view to building an estate of eco friendly homes with a combination of social housing starter homes to expensive private residencies. Their plan was to redevelop existing hospital buildings into luxury flats while retaining some for NHS use, the main part of the estate would be completely transformed by several hundred new homes.

Right in the middle of this development was Graylingwell Chapel, once used by the hospital, now virtually derelict and boarded up. We managed to do a deal with the then Homes & Communities Agency to re-open the chapel as a centre for the community and a sacred space for our church. We experienced something of a miracle.

At first the owners said we could use the building for an annual charge of £20,000. As a church we were sure that God was calling us to move into this building, so we continued to pursue our goal of moving in on Easter Sunday, 2010.

Shortly before we were due to move in, I had a call from the Home & Communities Agency saying they had changed their minds - they would be charging us a peppercorn rent of £2 per year!

We continued to pay this for the whole time that we were there in the chapel. And it did become a hub for the community with all kinds of activities taking place, including a 200 strong Community Choir running every Tuesday night.

As a Bishop's Mission in the Church of England, we had the flexibility to do church a little differently and drew people of all ages and backgrounds into a lively and growing church family.

But then it happened. It was bound to happen sooner or later.

After 10 years of ministry in this challenging but exciting situation, Sarah, who is also ordained as a priest in the Church of England, felt God calling her to further study in Oxford.

Her own journey following God's call on her life would fill a book all on its own. The challenges she had to overcome and the battles she faced would have been insurmountable to many, but she kept pressing forward and she was accepted into Oxford University to study for a Masters in Theology based at Wycliffe Hall.

Now we needed somewhere to live.

At my age it is far more likely that a House for Duty post in the Church of England would be a possibility, so that's what we were looking for within a 20 mile radius of Oxford. House for Duty is where you are able to live in a

Vicarage or Rectory, in return for giving two days a week plus Sundays to church ministry. This would enable Sarah to have a home base and present a new ministry challenge for me. Is it possible to look after two parish churches in two days a week plus Sundays? No, of course not! But that's another story.

Almost by chance we came across an advert for a House for Duty post in Quainton, just over 20 miles from Oxford. Even before I made a formal application, we drove into Buckinghamshire to visit the village. We remember very well driving up Station Road into the Village, turning right then left by the Village Green as we searched for the church. At the top of the Green we turned right into Church Street and there it was!

As soon as we arrived, we knew this was to be our new home. Perhaps a little presumptuous, but there was something about this place that felt right to us. We walked into the church and felt the presence of God there - the building steeped in history, where tens of thousands of people have worshipped and prayed, finding God, finding peace, finding forgiveness and new life.

Someone once said that the way you can tell if God is speaking to you, is that your heart starts beating a little faster! Well, it was just like that. However, the thing that really convinced us was a verse from the Bible which has followed me in every change in my life over the years. It's Isaiah 43:19 and it popped up again as we were considering the next move for our lives: "See, I am doing a new thing! Now it springs up; do you not perceive it? I am making a way in the wilderness and streams in the wasteland. Quainton and Oving, here we come!

4 THE JOKE ABOUT THE HORSE AND DESCARTES

What came over me?

There I was, having been shortlisted for the position of House for Duty Team Vicar in the Schorne Team of churches, with responsibility for two beautiful rural parishes, sitting with fifteen of my interviewers over lunch on the day of my interview and out popped the joke!

To be fair, it was probably because I didn't feel I had any chance of getting the job.

After all, the second person shortlisted was an accomplished vicar with years of experience in traditional church. And I'm sitting there, bald head, earring, with a slight Cockney twang, no experience in traditional church, let alone rural ministry, without any real idea about how things work in these parts.

It's like when you first fall in love with someone you really want to have a relationship with, but at first, the whole situation is rather intimidating and overwhelming and you end up saying ridiculous things to try to impress them!

First encounters like this are normally memorable for all the wrong reasons, but never very impressive!

The interview process was over two days and involved meeting various people, including the "competition" who was chaperoned along with me by the Rural Dean who spoke enthusiastically and realistically about the opportunities, challenges and expectations awaiting the newly appointed Team Vicar. On the first evening we shared a meal together in a local restaurant accompanied by Parochial Church Council members of the two parish churches concerned and clergy colleagues in the Schorne Team.

The meal was great, the conversation stimulating and the people interesting and interested in the both of us. Sarah, my wife, joined me and we stayed overnight in the delightful home of one of the Church Wardens and his wife.

The second day was interview day and lasted several hours, with various groups of people involved in the interviewing process. We had been asked to present a five minute reflection on verses from Jesus' prayer in John 17. It came to my turn and I dispensed with notes and clutching my big black Bible, spoke from the heart. It has always been my custom to prepare well, rehearse well and remember bullet points to which I attach the salient points of my talk - rather like using pegs to hang clothes of all shapes and sizes on a washing line. It seemed to go well, although I worried that I may have been a little informal in my approach.

Oh well! If you try to be something you really are not, people know it immediately. I could only be me, as inadequate as that might be.

Then came lunch and the inevitable joke! I know you want to hear it!

A horse walks into a bar. The bartender asks the horse if he's an alcoholic considering all the bars he visits, to which the horse replies "I don't think I am." And suddenly, POOF! The horse disappears. Now if you are into philosophy you would know about Descarte's proposition of cogito ergo sum - "I think, therefore I am." But if I had told you the meaning of the joke at the beginning, that would have been putting Descartes before the horse.

Yes, I know! And the miraculous thing is - I got the job!

5 THANK GOD FOR RECYCLED FURNITURE

As mentioned in an earlier reflection, my job at Quainton and Oving with Pitchcott is House For Duty Team Vicar.

At my ripe old age, House For Duty is the most likely new job you could hope for in the Church of England. It means exactly what it says. You get to live in a lovely Church of England Vicarage or Rectory in return for giving two days a week plus Sundays to the ministry of the church. No salary/stipend. This was perfect for us, with me on my State Pension and an amazing base for Sarah to work from.

I know what you're thinking. How can you look after two parish churches on two days a week plus Sundays? And the answer is - you can't! But that really doesn't bother me because I find ministry so fulfilling and a real privilege.

The real issue for us was furniture. We didn't have much and we had a five bedroom house to populate!

Not a bad problem to have.
In our previous church in Chichester, we lived in a small end of terrace house on an ex council housing estate near to the University. Lots of student Let's, loads of people living in challenging circumstances, some private homes but mostly rented. Although the house was small, it was definitely God's place for us. We were at the heart of the community to which God had called us. And unbeknown to us at the time, we had moved within 200 yards of

Graylingwell Chapel, a decommissioned NHS Chapel which had been disused for 13 years.

A perfect location to plant a church!

We had some memorable community events on the green at the front of our house. Every year the church would pitch up and we would run a Christmas Street Party with all the trimmings and in the summer we'd run another Street Party with live music, stalls and activities for the children. We became a hub for the community.

Space in our house was an issue. Our office for most of the time we were there, was in a 12' by 8' shed at the bottom of the garden, kindly donated by my wonderful mother-in-law.

Arriving in the Quainton and moving into a five bedroomed Rectory was amazing if not a little daunting. We had nowhere near enough furniture - not even a dining room table and chairs. However, we were soon directed to a used furniture warehouse in Aylesbury run by the Florence Nightingale Hospice.

We picked up a very nice dining room table with chairs for £60, three beds, including a double king size for a spare guest room, various useful bits and pieces for the kitchen, living room and study. We even picked up a coffee maker for £5 which we use almost every day. All good to go! And all proceeds for the amazing work of the Hospice. Now, with a good base to work from, we started to learn more about our patch. And one of the first things we discovered, was the story of the devil in a boot! That comes next!

6 THE DEVIL IN A BOOT!

As a newly appointed Team Vicar in the Schorne Team of churches, I was intrigued by the story of the devil in a boot!

And so it was that we drove to the nearby village of North Marston to see the shrine set up to commemorate the extraordinary life of John Schorne, a man of great faith, who exercised supernatural powers around these Buckinghamshire villages 700 years ago.

John was rector of the church at North Marston in 1282 and his fame spread far and wide after it was reported that during a time of drought, he struck the ground with his staff and a spring of water came pouring out, thus saving the village. The water was found to have healing properties and was particularly effective in curing gout, which was a common and painful disease of the day.

So amazing was this incident that the news even reached the court of King Henry VIII who suffered from gout himself. He must have been convinced by the story, because he made at least two pilgrimages to the shrine in North Marston, which is located by a well where it is thought that the spring first appeared.

But what about the devil in a boot?

Gout typically starts in the foot and was described in the middle ages as 'the devil in a boot.' Thus, at the shrine to this day, there is a depiction of the devil being thrown out of a boot. This image became associated with John

Schorne up until his death in 1314 and continues to this day.

By the 1400's, pilgrimages to the Holy Well in North Marston became the third most popular pilgrimage in England. Schorne's bones were moved to St George's Chapel, Windsor in 1478, but the story of his remarkable life lives on.

I don't like labels.

We tend to put people in boxes depending on their 'churchmanship.' If you wanted to pin a label on me, call me a card carrying fully paid up member of the evangelical charismatic brigade! This has been my emphasis over the years as I've tried to serve God in various ways.

So the thought of being Team Vicar in the Schorne Team of churches is quite exciting for me! We have a heritage dating back 700 years to a man who saw God at work and wasn't afraid to wear his faith on his collar and kick the devil out of a boot!

But what about the little yellow ducks?

That comes next!

7 THE LITTLE YELLOW DUCKS

Drivers in Buckinghamshire!

They are nuts!

I'm not a slow driver. I rode my XTZ 750 at 120 miles an hour several times and my trusted Volvo packs a fair punch. Since picking up a couple of speeding fines, I have mended my ways!

But the drivers around Aylesbury and the beautiful surrounding villages are something else!

I enjoy driving, but not so much in these parts!

I used to drive long distances, hours on end on the highways of America and the motorways and autobahns of Europe.

Every New Year, for several years, I was resident musician for the German Youth For Christ Conference in Nuremberg Castle. Great location overlooking the city. Always a family treat to climb to the top of the building and watch the fireworks at the stroke of 12 midnight.

So we all piled in the transit, fitted with three old aircraft seats in the back and a 1000 watt PA and lighting rig stacked to the rear and we'd drive the 2 hours to the ferry and then 5 hours across France and into Germany. It was an annual pilgrimage.

But that's nothing compared to the time I had to make a dash through the night from Copenhagen to Oostend to catch the ferry in time to preach at the morning service at a church in Kent.

So I'm not afraid of the accelerator! But it worries me that I have to drive defensively around here to protect myself from being run off the road by some lunatic trying to impress his girlfriend!

But there is something else that worries me - it worries me alot. The potholes.

I've never known anything like it. Protests have been made, notably by one gentleman in a village not too far away from here.

One rainy day, when all the potholes around the village were filled with water, he floated 100 yellow plastic ducks in the little pools created by the potholes. You might well be wondering... where did he get 100 yellow plastic ducks? And the answer: they were left over from the village fete. The sight was hilarious, and made a powerful statement. It hit local news and went viral on YouTube! The local authority soon jumped into action!

And that true story gives me a great illustration when I'm talking to young couples getting married.

In every relationship potholes occur.

Challenges and difficulties, disagreements and fallings out. It's a normal part of navigating life together. I know where all the potholes are in the villages around here, so I can avoid them. The worst thing we can do in our relationships however, is to ignore the potholes and simply navigate around them.

That's why it has been known for me to present two little yellow plastic ducks to the happy couple on their wedding day with the following instructions: when a pothole appears in your marriage, whichever partner feels unhappy or aggrieved should put their yellow plastic ducks in a prominent place in the home so that when their partner comes in, they will know immediately that there is something to deal with!

It's amazing the inspiration you can get from village life!

But what about the ancient monuments in church? No, I'm not talking about the people! I'm talking about places of worship being filled with historical memorials of those days gone my.

What's the value in them?

More about that coming up!

8 SEVEN HUNDRED YEARS WITH GOD AT WORK

I've always been fascinated by old buildings.

If I hadn't felt called into full time Christian ministry, I would have become an architect.

As a teenager I had a collection of books all about Roman and Greek architecture and I loved learning about the differences between Ionic, Doric and Corinthian columns. I was given a draughtsman's drawing board and quickly learned how to draw house plans whilst being careful to refer to local building regulations. To this day, there are at least two buildings still standing on the Isle of Sheppey that I designed and drew plans for as a teenager.

Sarah and I have been members of the National Trust for years. When my children were young, there may have been occasions when they didn't appreciate looking around another 'ancient relic', but now, at least one of my children has taken the plunge and is herself a member, along with her family.

One of the interesting things about coming to Quainton and Oving was the extraordinary history attached to the church buildings. The first time we talked into Quainton Church, the sense of history was tangible. But more than that, in both All Saints, Oving and Holy Cross and St Mary Quainton, God has been at work in these for more than 700 years. That's quite something.

Within the walls of these churches, which were built to the glory of God, people have found acceptance, forgiveness, hope, love, peace and new life as the work of the church has impacted the communities around them.

What a privilege to continue the tradition.

It seems possible that the Order of Knights Hospitaller were responsible for the 1340 rebuilding of Quainton church, on the site of an earlier church with roots in the Saxon period.

The Hospitallers are also credited with building the preaching cross that stands on the village green. They appeared in the early 11th century, during the time of the Benedictine Reform, as a group of individuals associated with an Amalfitan hospital in Jerusalem where they provided care for the sick, poor or injured pilgrims who travelled to the Holy Land. This Catholic organisation was influenced by the effects of the Reformation in Europe and many became Protestants as a result, expanding into England and developing their desire to serve the poor and needy.

The main feature of interest at Quainton is the large number of historic monuments that crowd the interior. Among these are fascinating memorials of the Dormer and Pigott families, as well as a lovely monument to Dr Richard Brett, one of the scholars responsible for translating the King James Bible. Dr Brett served as rector of Quainton for 42 years before his death in 1637. There are several memorial brasses, the earliest of which is to an unnamed girl (died c. 1360). There are further brasses to a priest (d. 1422), and a local man (d. 1510). In the north aisle is a monument to Richard Winwood (c. 1689), who founded a row of almshouses in the village that still stand today. Winwood's statue is shown reclining and dressed in armour.

All Saints, Oving is the oldest building in the village, dating back to the 13th century. An earlier wooden church was probably on the site. The nave, chancel, lancets and north and south aisles are 13th century, the East Chapel is 14th century and the tower was completed in 1674. Local tradition has it that Oliver Cromwell watered his horses in a spring near the church and the village would have seen Royalists and Roundheads passing through, sometimes taking refuge from their opponents in the church building.

It's a privilege to serve the church and community within such a rich historical tradition and to discover new ways to communicate the unchanging Gospel message which is at the heart of all we do.

Anyway - I was soon to face the question: to chasuble or not to chasuble? I settled on a solution. Coming up next!

9 TO CHASUBLE OR NOT TO CHASUBLE?

When I first started out as a Baptist Minister at South Ashford Baptist Church in Kent, I wore a full clerical collar. Never wore robes, but always quite smartly dressed. After five years at the church I embarked on an itinerant music ministry - that was in 1978. I released my first album, Freefall, in 1979 on the Kingsway Music label.

So naturally my dress code changed dramatically! I remember with some embarrassment, taking the main stage with my band at the wonderful Greenbelt Festival, dressed in 'hippy' gear. It may have been cool at the time, but not by today's standards. Mind you, walking through Oxford City centre and observing what people wear, can be a real eye popping moment. It seems like today, anything goes!

Then there was the hair style! I used to have long dark hair with blonde streaks and 'beaded rat tails' hanging down the back! A good friend, Rachel, used to do my hair and I remember on occasions sitting at home with a plastic bag on my head, through which she would pull strands of hair and using some rather toxic substance, cover the strands thoroughly, and turning them blonde. I'm sure she still has a picture secretly stashed away somewhere of me in this rather embarrassing state and I'm hoping it never sees the light of day!

Of course, in those days I'd be looking out for any fashionable gear that you could constitute as being 'cool' for my concert performances.

I can't remember ever wearing a suit for anything - apart from at the wedding services of my kids. It was all black leather, black T-shirts and ripped jeans. You can still buy ripped jeans these days - they have never gone out of fashion.

Clerical clothing is an interesting subject and we all have our own views on what vicars should or shouldn't wear. I don't think I've ever seen a church leader or vicar in one of the HTB churches wearing clerical gear. And certainly, when I, together with Sarah, was called back into a pastoral church based ministry in Chichester, we never wore dog collars or any other form of clerical gear. I sometimes wore a dog collar for hospital visiting - the uniform gets you in to see people at any time of the day or night - with an ID card obviously. And for some, it brings some degree of comfort to see a 'proper vicar.'

So when I landed the job as Team Vicar in Quainton and Oving, there was an expectation that I would wear clerical garments...dog collar (obviously), cassock, surplice, preaching scarf, different coloured stoles according to the changing liturgical colours of the church year - green, red, white and purple and a cassock-alb when presiding at Holy Communion.

There is a well-stocked wardrobe in my vestry at church and in them are a number of chasubles and cassocks, donated by various clergy through the years. A chasuble is an ornate sleeveless outer vestment often worn by Catholic or High Anglican priests when presiding at Holy Communion.

I took the decision very early on in my ministry at Quainton and Oving, that I would wear a chasuble, which would be a step too far for many of my colleagues, particularly the evangelical brigade. I made this decision out of respect for my people, who found this sign of my priestly role helpful and engaging.

Dress code is important in the particular setting into which God has called me and gives me an opportunity to demonstrate that I am a servant of the people and a servant of God.

A chasuble is one thing, but sung evensong, rock style? Find out what happened - coming up next!

10 LIKE A ROCK 'N ROLL SINGER!

I'm taking a risk making the following public! That might sound overly dramatic but I have my reputation at stake after all! It's takes a lot to shock me these days, I've seen it all, bought the T-shirt and the fridge magnet, so when the day came that I realised what I'd let myself in for, it did come as a shock.

We all remember things that made us stop in our tracks. The are usually things that we don't expect and that we are suddenly confronted with. I've been round the block enough times to know that life is never black and white and there are various shades of grey in terms of the way people live their lives. I've seen extremely traumatic things that have shocked me, like watching a baying crowd urging a young man to jump off a high building in Bombay or meeting a lady who had lived on the street outside a Baptist Missionary Society Home in abject poverty. She had lived there for 38 years.

Then there have been the more trivial "shocking" experiences like the time I was thanked for a concert I performed at a girl's school in Reigate. The rather naive Christian teacher thanked me by saying, "Well girls, obviously Mr Flashman has something that we haven't got," referring to my Christian faith of course, but it didn't come over like that to the girls!

Anyway, back to the story in hand. I was sitting in my priests's stall at one of my first services in Quainton, and my colleague, sitting opposite me, suddenly started singing the liturgy. It was Sung Evensong. Now, you might not think that is such a big deal, but the fact is, although I was expecting a service of Evensong, I hadn't realised it was 'Sung'! I had no idea what I was doing. The best part was everybody else thought I knew exactly what I was doing. I'm the Vicar after all!

It is amazing that if you look like you know what you are doing, everybody thinks that's they way it should be. It's just your special style!

Anyway, fortunately John, sitting opposite me, led really well and all I had to do was preach. So I just sat there looking spiritual and Vicar-like and joined in where I could.

I've been in Christian ministry most of my adult life and worked in a variety of settings, but this was totally new to me. I should have known this, but for some reason the penny didn't drop!

After my initial shock and a degree of panic, I got together with Geoffrey, our very wonderful and accomplished organist, and he taught me how to sing the liturgy for Evensong. So armed with the music in front of me, I was ready and prepared for my first experience of leading Sung Evensong. I led the service a few weeks later and it seemed to go really well. The call and response by our equally wonderful robed choir led the congregation in meaningful worship. Back home after the service, I was feeling rather pleased with myself and asked my lovely wife Sarah how I did. She said, "darling, it was note perfect. But you sang like a rock 'n roll singer!"

"Vicar! Someone's trying to kill me!"

More about that coming up…

11 SOMEONE'S TRYING TO KILL ME!

A few short weeks after arriving in Quainton I got a phone call from a local man. "Are you the new vicar?" "Yes, I am, how can I help?" "What shall I call you vicar?" "Call me Steve. Now how can I help?"

"Steve, can you come round straight away, someone is trying to kill me!"

My wife Sarah and I have been confronted with all kinds of pastoral situations over the years. Family break-ups. Bigamy. People struggling with gender identity. Trying to support families facing with the loss of a loved one.

Offering a safe place for people rejected by those who should be supporting and caring for them. Picking up the pieces of people's broken lives for reasons, often no fault of their own.

Dealing with the trauma that many people are faced with through bereavement, loss, divorce and separation or the death of a child.

However, I was worried when I got the call from this person who was obviously distressed and in fear of losing his life. I've never had to deal with a potential murder on my own doorstep!

"I'm just nipping down the road for a minute darling," I said to Sarah, as I walked out the front door, making sure she knew the address where I was going.

In rural ministry, you need to know your demographic.

What kind of people live in your patch? Age group? Young families? Older folk? Commuters? Social and cultural background? Education?

All this enables you to begin to pray through appropriate ways to connect with people where they're at. A colleague of mine many years ago said to me, "Steve, the problem with many theologians these days is that they are answering questions that no-one is asking."

Very true.

So off I went, walking through the village at quite a pace, wondering what I would encounter following the rather dramatic telephone call. I had my mobile phone at the ready, in case I needed to phone the police or the emergency services.

One of the delightful things about village life, is that it can take 30 minutes to get to the shop, which is only 3 minutes away. If there are people around, it's quite the normal thing to stop and have a chat.

But not today!

I don't often run anywhere these days, but I can get up quite a fast walking pace when I'm in a hurry. And today I was in a hurry!

When I reached my destination I met this rather charming elderly gentleman who was receiving a lot of support from his family, but had somehow got it into his head that someone was trying to kill him.

But knowing the family as I do, nothing could be further from the truth.

Dementia is a crippling illness that affects not only the person going through it, but also family and friends who feel as if they are losing a loved one prematurely.

However close you may have been to someone, the distance between you grows as the days and weeks reveal a gradual deterioration in physical and mental health and a loss of mobility.

It's heartbreaking and demeaning for all concerned.

All I could do was to offer some prayers, give reassuring advice and ongoing support and try to walk the journey with those concerned.

I am continually struck by the privilege I have of getting alongside people in the critical and celebratory times in their lives.

But then I was called into the home of a dying man who didn't do God, Church or vicars.

The outcome became one of the most memorable moments of the last 3 years.

Coming up next.

12 HE DOESN'T DO GOD, CHURCH OR VICARS!

In my first year as Team Vicar, I conducted 28 funerals.

I look after three open churchyards, one in Quainton, one in Pitchcott and one in Oving. All three are in beautiful locations and the sense of the presence of God is tangible.

So much so, that people often sit in one of the churchyards and have a time of reflection and prayer. These sanctified places give us a sense of our own mortality, but also the abundant grace and mercy of God.

The words of God, "Do not be afraid," feature many times in the Bible, notably just before and after the death and resurrection of Jesus, when He said to His followers, "Let not your heart be troubled, neither let them be afraid."

These words of Jesus lead me often into a funeral service, where I can offer hope, peace and a future to the bereaved as we leave their loved ones in the safe hands of a living God.

I often come across people who say to me, "I don't do God, church or vicars, but you do, so could you say a prayer for me."

It's interesting that many people still have a sense of "something else" beyond themselves. Or to use the strap line from the Alpha Course, "Is there more to life than this?"

Many people I meet, particularly in and around the villages, have a sense that there is more to life than this. They don't translate that into church going, but they love the church and like to think of it as their own.

And so it was, that shortly after arriving in Quainton I was called by a lovely lady who told me about her sick husband. "Can I come and see him?" I asked. "You can try," she said, "but he doesn't do church or vicars, or God."

I was invited into the house and sat down opposite this delightful elderly gentleman. I was wearing my dog collar. "Hello (name)," I said, "My name's Steve, I'm the new vicar."

"I know who you are," was the rather brusque reply! "Tell me about your life," I asked in as friendly a way I could muster.

He looked rather bemused and then catching on to the idea, started telling me his life story, which was fascinating. An hour and a half later, he came to the end of his story.

I then asked if I could pray with him before leaving. "OK, why not," he said. I prayed for him and his wife and left.

He asked me back again a couple of weeks later and then again a few days before he died. I was able to talk to him about God's love for him and we said the Lord's Prayer together. Before I left he said to me, "I do believe you know."

It was an encounter I will never forget and taught me so much about listening, not jumping to conclusions about people and enabling those at the end of their life, to reach out with a simple faith and take hold of God's loving hand.

13. SMASHING THE MYTH

Like so many people I have met over the years, I had a very distorted view of the Anglican Church.

I was convinced that most people who called themselves C of E were not real Christians because on the rare occasions when they would actually turn up at church, they would perform weird religious rituals that didn't mean anything in the grand scheme of things. For me, this was a million miles away from the life giving and life fulfilling design of God for our lives.

Anyway, if ticking all the right boxes gets you to heaven, I'm definitely in! I was christened at St Luke's Church, West Norwood in South London. Then I was baptised by full immersion in the Baptist Church at age 14. And much later in life I was Confirmed in Chichester Cathedral.
And my professional Christian credentials are just as impressive!

I was Ordained as a Baptist Minister after 4 years of rigorous academic training at Spurgeon's Theological College in London, taking exams through the London University.

Then in my late 50's, jumped ship and was Ordained into the Anglican Church. Quite a journey. But of course, you and I both know that all of this doesn't guarantee me a place in heaven!

My earliest memory of 'real' church was Chatsworth Baptist Church, where my parents ended up, my dad having found faith under the powerful ministry of Baptist Minister, Revd Frank Goodwin.

Incidentally, Frank had a profound effect on my own emerging faith as a child, his preaching was vibrant, powerful, relevant and challenging and his prayers were spoken from the heart - no script required!

It wasn't until after leaving theological training as a Baptist Minister, that I became aware that something extraordinary was going on in the Anglican Church led by towering figures such as David Watson, Vicar of St Michael le Belfrey in York.

David was one of the first ministers to welcome John Wimber, a prominent Vineyard Church leader from America to the UK, bringing with him the creative and influential Charismatic Movement into mainstream Anglicanism.

When I had the chance to attend a week long ministers conference led by David in York, I jumped at the chance and found my stereotypical view of the Anglican Church smashed to pieces. The week I spent there formed the foundation for much of my future ministry.

And later in life I would find myself working alongside many God-centred and Spirit filled priests, vicars and bishops who's lives were focused on the holiness of God and His mission in the world.

However, I still struggled with certain kinds of churchmanship within the Anglican Church. I also struggled with the many people I met who wanted their babies christened, without having any sense of a personal commitment to Christ themselves or any real awareness of the promises they would make on behalf of their child. This was certainly true of my dad, when he had me christened at St Luke's. It was the done thing.

This still bothers me.

But then it happened! I landed the job of Team Vicar with responsibility for two traditional village churches and I imagined I would be like a fish out of water.

To be honest, at first I WAS like a fish out of water! But I soon found myself jumping in lock, stock and barrel as I started to encounter 'traditional' Anglicans who had a deep and profound faith in God and a prayer life to go with it.

Notably this happened when I went to visit an older couple, who, in another time and place I would have viewed suspiciously as people with little or no knowledge of God. I was shocked as they told me that they prayed for me and Sarah every day, that they prayed for the village and the church regularly and they were just completing the Bible In A Year course with Nicky Gumbel of Holy Trinity Brompton! I felt ashamed that I could be so judgemental.

Since those days, I have come to know and appreciate many deeply committed Christian folk in the villages that I serve and they have given me a lesson I needed to learn. We all have our own spiritual journey, and we can learn so much from others who might express their faith differently, but that doesn't mean they are less spiritual or second class Christians.

My distorted view of traditional Anglicanism smashed. Up next: Matt Redman versus Hymns Ancient and Modern!

14 MATT REDMAN VERSUS ANCIENT & MODERN

I haven't sung so many traditional hymns since my childhood!

And, you know what, it's been like a renaissance for me. We have such a rich musical heritage from some astounding hymn writers who had a profound sense of the holiness and glory of God.

In my parish churches we have a variety of services, some using contemporary worship songs and others using traditional hymns and I've come to value both.

I've got to be careful I don't get on my high horse at this point because one of the things that niggle me, alongside shopping trolleys with wobbly wheels and cafe tables with one leg shorter than the others - oh, and middle lane drivers on the motorway - extremely annoying - is what I perceive as the commercialisation of contemporary worship music.

A quick glance at Song Select, by far the biggest source of worship material in the world, run by Christian Copyright Licensing International, demonstrates simply by looking at the posed images of many our best loved worship leaders, how far down the road of commercialisation we have come.

Please don't get me wrong.

I know that the labourer is worthy of his pay, but over

the last decade or two, worship songs have generated millions of pounds and dollars worth of revenue through royalties and album sales worldwide.

It's concerning to me that some worship leaders seem to get inspired to write worship songs and release albums just before Christian Conference season begins, in time to pick up sales from devoted punters!

Without a doubt, there are some great worship songs out there which have been inspired by God and bring Him the glory.

Matt Redman's "Bless The Lord Oh My Soul" is one such classic and has been used to bring millions into the presence of God. And there are many more.

However, in my view, we do need to address this issue of commercialisation. I've been to many charismatic services - which I love by the way - but found that the worship band takes centre stage, in every meaning of that word.

Charles Wesley wrote more than 8000 hymns and travelled the country sharing his faith, and he didn't earn royalties and he didn't do photo shoots and he didn't sign autographs.

I know it was a different time and place, but I can't imagine he would have had any part in the commercialisation of his worship material if he were alive today. The money he did acquire, he swiftly gave to the poor and needy, which gave even more credence and credibility to the Gospel he was proclaiming.

He composed some of the most memorable and lasting hymns of the church: "Hark! The Herald Angels Sing," "And Can It Be," "O for a Thousand Tongues to Sing," "Love Divine, All Loves Excelling," "Jesus, Lover of My Soul," "Christ the Lord Is Risen Today."

Hymns that go right to the heart of the Gospel and raise our spirits in worship to God.

It was on Whitsunday, May 21, 1738, that Charles experienced an encounter with the Holy Spirit - it was God bringing him into contact with a personal pentecostal moment.

He wrote in his journal that the Spirit of God, "chased away the darkness of my unbelief." He later wrote a hymn to commemorate his day of salvation. There is some debate among scholars as to which of three hymns this was, but the most likely candidate is the hymn that asks, "And can it be that I should gain an interest in the Saviour's blood?"

The last verse triumphantly proclaims:

"No condemnation now I dread,
Jesus, and all in Him, is mine:
Alive in Him, my living Head,
And clothed in righteousness Divine,
Bold I approach th' eternal throne,
And claim the crown, through Christ, my own."

OK. I've got that one off my chest, now I've got to grapple with the church running a beer festival!

15. WHAT! THE CHURCH RUNS A BEER FESTIVAL!

One thing I've learned over the years is that I need to lighten up a little bit!

Christians can be - unhelpfully - intense about their faith.

Don't get me wrong! The foundations of our Christian faith are non negotiable, but the way we express our faith can take on different shapes and forms according to our cultural setting and the way we do church. So the way we do church in an urban setting would be very different from church in a rural setting.

Fairly obvious I know. But it takes a little time for the penny to drop with me!

When I heard that the church in Quainton ran a Beer Festival in the summer every year, I wondered what was going on. Beer Festival?

People enthused about it! Barrels of beer were donated by local business people and generous benefactors, the local pub would give space on the forecourt outside to sell the beer to the consuming public. There would be lots of stalls selling various things from bric a brac to G 'n T and there would be fun activities like a dog show and pram race. Obviously live music would be playing on the Green for most of the day with local bands strutting their stuff. All profits raised would be for the benefit of the church.

It didn't take me long to catch on to the idea! Not because I am in love with beer, although I quite like a pint now and then but because I witnessed that first summer the community coming together in large numbers, picnicking together, playing together, laughing together and generally having a good time. They applauded the dog show - especially the dog with the shaggiest tail - and showed appreciation to the solo artists and bands playing for their entertainment.

Of course! The rural communities are all about building relationships with neighbours, friends and family and being part of something together that, in the end, is meaningful, because it benefits the ongoing ministry of the church.

Almost from the word go I was roped in to take charge of the music and the last couple of years I have organised for a friendly local farmer to bring his large covered trailer which he carefully negotiates through the narrow country lanes from Oving to Quainton, and then sets up at the top of the Green ready for the live music soloists and bands to perform from 1.00pm to 10.00pm in the evening.

During my second year of managing the stage, I was leading our Community Choir on the trailer and was suddenly overcome with the heat. I felt myself falling and managed to hand my guitar to someone nearby as I went down.

Immediately, there was a flurry of activity from concerned onlookers all around me and quickly there was a medic on hand to sort me out. I hadn't been drinking enough water and had become very dehydrated. As I was helped off the stage, there was a round of applause and the relief from everybody was tangible.

That's village life for you. There is a genuine care for one another and if someone is in trouble, people come to help.

Then I had a dilemma - should I bless the chicken or say grace?

You'll find out in the next episode!

16. SHALL I BLESS THE CHICKEN, OR SAY GRACE?

I loved the Vicar of Dibley series on TV. So many memorable comedy moments. Dawn French falling down a hole in the ground thinking it was a small puddle!

Dawn French dressing up as an Easter Bunny to keep the village tradition going. Dawn French eating several Christmas dinners for fear of offending anybody. And how could we forgot Dawn French at the Pet Service!

A short time after arriving, my Parish Church in Oving announced they had organised a Pet Service on the village green. It was set up beautifully with a medium sized marquee, wonderful refreshments - especially the coffee and walnut cake! (To which I am treated on a regular basis by the way!)

Quite a few families came carrying or leading their pets to be blessed by the Vicar!

Before becoming a country Vicar, I would have dismissed a service like this and relegated it to the box marked "weird and absurd."

As a father and step-father, I have done my fair share of pet burials in various gardens, not just anybody's garden you understand!

And mainly guinea pigs, although I once tried to revive an ailing hamster by offering it a touch of brandy from a syringe. The poor little thing did respond for a while and was probably very happy when it finally left this world.

I've also had my fair share of awkward questions about animals in heaven and have come to the honest conclusion that it is unlikely that God would create such wonderful creatures, only to relegate them into oblivion.

I have a feeling the New Heaven And New Earth will be teeming with interesting and colourful creatures.

As the prophet Isaiah says, "the lion will lay down with the lamb..."
so I'm not just being a sentimental, pet loving, wishful thinking exponent of this idea. And I'm not just thinking about...

...Mary, Floppsy, Emily, Tom & Jerry, Millie & Harry, Biscuit, Fudge and Lightning, Lillie, Lou Lou, Pinkie, Rosie, Mimmie, Daisy, Binky Patch, Pepper, and Sweet Pea.

And of course our lovely dogs:

Paddy Wo Wo, Ruff, Tess, Jack, Freddie, Roxy and Molly, and not forgetting Albert the hedgehog and Harold the frog.

Anyway, I have been converted! Converted into seeing the great value of our annual Pet Service!

The community come together with the pets that mean so much to them, that bring such joy into their lives. They bring them because they care about them - and rightly so, they are God's creatures and deserve our respect and care. So I have no problem praying for God's creation and even pronouncing a blessing or two.

Then it happened!

I was not expecting it. It was my first Pet Service after all. A little girl came forward with a cardboard box and very carefully and lovingly opened the box to reveal her pet chicken.

To be honest with you, at that moment I didn't know whether to say grace or pray a blessing! "My chicken is not well," she said, looking up at me pleadingly. I took hold of the box, looking extremely Vicar-like, and after examining the poor creature, lifted my priestly hand and said grace - ooops, no I didn't mean that! I said a prayer of blessing on the unsuspecting chicken and off home it went with its satisfied owner.

Priceless!

These kinds of events build community by building relationships and that is what it's all about.

Call me the Vicar of Dibley all you like, but come along with me to the next Pet Service and see what a blessing it can be for all concerned.

17 THE VICAR GOT THE TURKEY!

I didn't mean to!

I wouldn't have bid for the turkey at the pub Harvest Auction if I had known that someone else always gets it!

It was only a couple of weeks after arriving in Quainton that one of the guys at the George And Dragon, our local pub, asked if I would open the Harvest Auction which was always held at the pub in the autumn and the vicar opens it.

Of course I said yes, and the big night came.

The pub was crammed, as it always is for community events like this one. I managed to elbow my way to the front and sat, ready for my big moment. The Auctioneer pushed a small step ladder in my direction and handed my a radio mic. I climbed the ladder and introduced myself. It was pretty obvious that I was the new vicar because I was wearing my dog collar - that's what you do in a village community.

I told some ridiculous joke - I think I said something like, "Hello everyone, I'm the new vicar and it's great to be with you. And by the way, this is not my real ladder, it's my step ladder." No - one laughed.

Early days. They are still checking me out.

Auction opened and out come all the exhibits - mostly

food and flowers. Boxes of bedding plants, huge marrows, prize onions and baskets of vegetables all hoisted in the air and the bidding begins.

Then came the star moment - it's the turkey, donated by a local family every year to raise money for local charities. I started bidding and couldn't stop!

I got the turkey!

For a few weeks after that the story went round the village. "The Vicar got the turkey!"

I didn't realise the significance of this until someone tipped me off.

Ole Mr So 'n So always gets the turkey.

I felt dreadful. I'm the new Vicar, trying to make a positive impression and I've blown it! I haven't even got my feet under the table, and already my reputation is seeping around the village - "The Vicar got the turkey!"

Fortunately people are very forgiving and we soon settled in to village life.

The following year at the Harvest Auction I'm there again, but not bidding for the turkey. I'm sitting near the front and again the place is crammed. Suddenly the auctioneer cried out an expletive! "Oi," I said, "enough of that language, but I forgive you," waving my hand in the shape of a cross in front of him. "Well done Vicar!" he cried, "you just won the bid for this beautiful plastic tiered cake stand!"

I went home that night with some bedding plants, a small carton of local beers and a plastic tiered cake stand!

The cake stand is still in its box in the garage.

Anyone want it?

18. FIVE SERVICES A DAY!

I have a habit of shooting myself in the foot!

It was entirely my own fault.
I had the best of intentions.
I really thought it would work out.
I clearly made a massive mis calculation.

Now to be honest with you, it might be that I was trying to be a little over zealous and dare I say it, trying to impress people with my dedication and spiritual stature.

I've fallen into the same trap several times in my life - well actually, many times in my life.

The thing is, it's not wrong to have a high work ethic - it's when you become a workaholic that you hit problems! That won't impress anybody and just gets you into trouble with the wife!

My father was the same, so I probably got the work bug from him. He was a hard working builder, decorator and worked for himself most of his life. He scraped together a reasonable living, although we lived in a downstairs rented flat in London when I was growing up.

No TV. No telephone. Outside loo. No bathroom. My mother would boil kettles of water and fill an old metal bath dragged in from the backyard and squeezing into the scullery, there I would have my bath once a week. The rest of the time it would be sitting in a massive old white sink and getting clean the best way I could.

So my father worked long hours to maintain what little we had. My mother worked too. She had an old bicycle with a basket on the front. We used to call them "Hallelujah bikes" in those days because they'd been made famous by the Dutch Reformed Church, the people of which used their bikes to cycle to Sunday worship.

She would cycle around the streets of London as a mobile hairdresser, cutting and perming the hair of her clients, whilst being quite "preachy" with them about her faith.

When you're cutting someone's hair, you've got a captive audience for an hour or two!

So that's my excuse! Blame it in the parents!

No not really - we all have to take personal responsibility for our lives and stop blaming other people.

So I confess - it was my own fault.

"What?" You may well ask. I'll come to that in a minute.

Being busy and doing things can lead us into another pitfall.

We can easily mistake who we are by what we do. And of course what we do doesn't define us. It might explain things about us, but it's not who we are. And my problem for many years was that I compared Filofaxes with my colleagues and had to make sure that mine contained more diary entries than anyone else.

I still use a Filofax by the way. But I digress.

And so it was that after arriving here in Quainton and Oving I discovered that, in both churches there were some Sundays where there was no morning service or no evening service.

Shocking! I was brought up to go to church every Sunday morning, every Sunday evening and Sunday School in the afternoon at 3.00pm.

So fairly quickly I filled in the gaps.

It meant that some Sundays I was leading and preaching at five services. 8.00am Holy Communion, Book of Common Prayer in Quainton, followed by a 9.30am Family Service. The off to Oving where I led an 11.00am Family Service followed by a 5.00pm Holy Communion or Evensong. Then back to Quainton for a 6.30pm Evensong or Holy Communion.

After a few months of this, I wore myself out!

Surprised?

Now, with the help and wisdom of both PCC's - for those not versed in Church of England governance, PCC is the Parochial Church Council - a bit like Deacons would be in some churches or Elders in others - I have come to a sensible and workable service rota. Still busy, but manageable!

Up next: Show em your cross!

19. SHOW 'EM YOUR CROSS!

You have too learn quickly in these parts!

For instance, you don't call the standard carried by the Royal British Legion, a flag. That's a big "no no" and of course, incorrect. I referred to them in this way once, and was very promptly corrected!

Quite right!

As a boy growing up in London I joined the Boys Brigade which was connected to our church, and we would parade down Norwood High Street once a month, wearing the distinctive navy blue uniform, pillbox hat, short trousers and one inch white canvas belt with the appropriate BB Buckle, together with buglers and drummers making quite a racket I can tell you.

Not sure how much it was appreciated on a Sunday morning!

I remember the parade very well, because we always marched past the flats where Jean Springate lived - a childhood sweetheart. Although I never spoke to her - it was a kind of long distance love affair. I always hoped she'd lean out of her window as we were passing in our smart uniforms and somehow notice me and perhaps blow a kiss!

Never happened.

One of the big events of the year in our villages is Remembrance Sunday, and a lot of people come to church to pay their respects to those who sacrificed so much during times of conflict.

The Royal British Legion play a prominent part in the proceedings. They carry a lot of respect from us because of their support for the Armed Forces, and veterans and their families. Their support continues through life, offering help to those often traumatised by the scars of war.

Remembrance Sunday is also one of the occasions when, together with the choir and uniformed organisations, we have a grand procession into the church being ably led by our cross bearer, Nicki.

On November 11th, 2018, more than 1,200 beacons were lit across England to mark the 100th anniversary of the end of the First World War.

Our village of Quainton was one of those locations and we had the privilege of lighting our beacon on Mill Hill overlooking the village.

Leading up to this memorable moment, we had our Remembrance Service in church and then processed through the village to the Memorial Hall for a reception.

There were a lot of people on the road, including the uniformed organisations and the Royal British Legion carrying the Standards - Nicki was leading carrying the cross.

Suddenly a few cars appeared and we were in danger of being mown down. Someone shouted from the back of the procession, "Nicki! Show 'em your cross!" At which we all fell about laughing!

Later in the evening, several hundred people gathered on Mill Hill and after a short speech from the Vicar - that's me! - and some prayers, the Beacon was lit.

And very impressive it was too!

That's all well and good, but how am I going to get the people singing, Sha La La??

Up next!

20 YOU'LL NEVER GET THEM SINGING 'SHA LA LA!'

It all started with a dream!

It was 2010 and our church had moved into Graylingwell Chapel in Chichester. It was such a memorable day. I've written elsewhere about the miracle of how we were able to set up church here, but just to say that leading up to this day, Easter 2010, we saw God do some amazing things.

This disused chapel had been standing there for 13 years and subsequently was in quite a state. No electricity, hence no lighting or heating. One of our members happened to pass a skip outside a local school with a dumped lighting rig sticking out of it. He got permission to grab it for the church and a few days later it was up in the church with a temporary electrical connection which local builders put in for us.

So now we were in the heart of a growing community.

I don't often watch Songs of Praise on TV. But on this one occasion I was inspired by a Welsh choir singing Guide Me O Thou Great Redeemer to an amazing arrangement accompanied by lighting effects. It looked and sounded amazing.

That night, much to the surprise of my long suffering wife, I sat bolt upright in bed singing, Guide Me O Thou Great Redeemer - and I had been dreaming about it!

I resolved the next day to start a Community Choir and within weeks we had a choir of 200 local people singing every Tuesday night in the Chapel, pop, rock, gospel and soul music - accompanied by me on guitar and with the help of a conductor who led proceedings.

Community Choirs UK was born and soon we had seven choirs running in West Sussex.

On moving to Quainton, I felt that a community choir would be a great thing to bring people together. I was expecting a turn out of perhaps 15 or 20 people at our Friday morning slot booked at the local Memorial Hall. But on the first rehearsal day we had more than 30 people and it has maintained numbers ever since.

"You'll never get them singing 'She La La'" said Sarah before the first rehearsal. Not only did they love singing pop, rock and gospel, the choir thrived and grew. And people of different ages and backgrounds all came together to sing their hearts out.

It's a joy to see people gaining in confidence and finding their voice in a stress free zone.

Now we have two choirs running, one in Waddesdon and one in Quainton and both choirs are thriving. We hold regular concerts and have raised hundreds of pounds for local charities.

I've come to appreciate the value of community and building meaningful relationships with people from all backgrounds. It's been an incredible experience and long may it continue.

Coming Up In The Next Book In The Series:

1. The Pony, The Plough And The Morris Dancers
2. Where Do All The Charismatics Go?
3. Dancing With My iPad In The Chancel
4. Fender Strat In Quainton School
5. Rock Music In Church – But Will They Come?
6. Victorian Pews And A Grand Banquet
and a lot more!

ABOUT THE AUTHOR, STEVE FLASHMAN

He is ordained in the Anglican Church, but started out as a Baptist, completing four years theological training at Spurgeon's Theological College in London, England. After serving as a Baptist Pastor in Ashford, Kent, he travelled the world as a Singer/Songwriter, Author, TV and Radio Presenter and Preacher, performing in hundreds of venues across the world, from the Streets of San Francisco, to the slums of Calcutta; Wembley Arena in London, England (the home of English football) to schools, prisons and clubs around Europe; The Marquee Club in Soho, where some of the most famous bands in the world have performed, to the Barrios of South America; the Killing Fields of Cambodia to the Kibera Slum in Nairobi; the Royal Albert Hall in London, England to the Sagrada Familia in Barcelona. The main focus of his music was in "grass roots" ministry – schools, colleges, universities, pubs, clubs and prisons – often speaking and performing to hundreds of people every week.

Printed in Great Britain
by Amazon

MURDER AT THE GRAND NATIONAL

A LADY ELIZABETH HAWTHORNE MYSTERY

OLIVIA ROSE

Copyright © 2024 by Olivia Rose

All rights reserved.

No part of this publication may be reproduced, distributed, or transmitted in any form or by any means, including photocopying, recording, or other electronic or mechanical methods, without the prior written permission of the publisher, except as permitted by U.S. copyright law. For permission requests, contact [include publisher/author contact info].

The story, all names, characters, and incidents portrayed in this production are fictitious. No identification with actual persons (living or deceased), places, buildings, and products is intended or should be inferred.

Publisher: Olivia Rose

Editor: Emily Lawrence (**Lawrence Editing)**

Lady Elizabeth Hawthorne – Family Tree

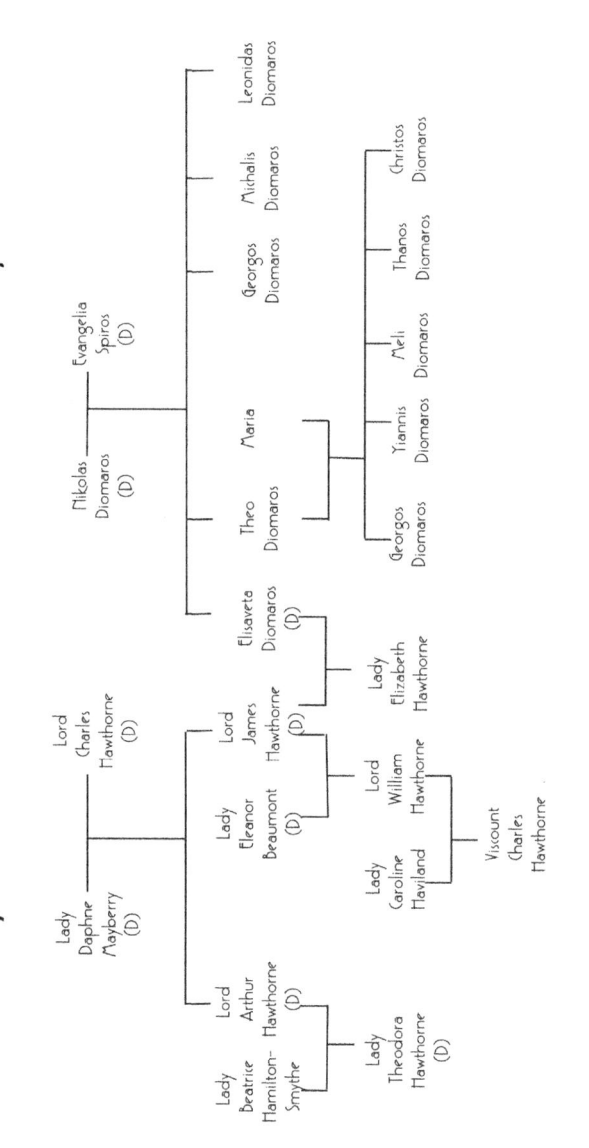

Hawthorne Side

- Lady Beatrice Hamilton-Smythe — Lord Arthur Hawthorne (D)
  - Lady Theodora Hawthorne (D)

- Lady Daphne Mayberry (D) — Lord Charles Hawthorne (D)
  - Lady Eleanor Beaumont (D) — Lord James Hawthorne (D) — Elisaveta Diomaros (D)
    - Lady Caroline Hayland — Lord William Hawthorne
      - Viscount Charles Hawthorne
    - Lady Elizabeth Hawthorne

Diomaros Side

- Nikolas Diomaros (D) — Evangelia Spiros (D)
  - Elisaveta Diomaros (D)
  - Theo Diomaros
  - Maria
    - Georgos Diomaros
    - Yiannis Diomaros
    - Meli Diomaros
    - Thanos Diomaros
    - Christos Diomaros
  - Georgos Diomaros
  - Michalis Diomaros
  - Leonidas Diomaros

Contents

Chapter One	1
Chapter Two	12
Chapter Three	27
Chapter Four	41
Chapter Five	54
Chapter Six	66
Chapter Seven	77
Chapter Eight	91
Chapter Nine	105
Chapter Ten	120
Chapter Eleven	133
Chapter Twelve	151
Chapter Thirteen	163
Chapter Fourteen	176

Chapter Fifteen	196
Chapter Sixteen	212
Chapter Seventeen	227
Chapter Eighteen	240
Chapter Nineteen	254
Chapter Twenty	270
Chapter Twenty-One	284
Chapter Twenty-Two	295
Chapter Twenty-Three	305
Chapter Twenty-Four	315
Epilogue	324
Dedication	332
Also by Olivia Rose	333
About the Author	342

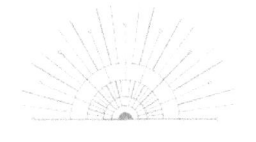

Chapter One

T HE TRAIN LURCHED FORWARD, its wheels clacking against the iron tracks as it pulled away from Liverpool Lime Street Station. Elizabeth leaned closer to the window, her hazel eyes drinking in the changing landscape. The densely packed, bustling city melted away, giving way to the lush, verdant fields of rural Lancashire.

Elizabeth exhaled, the tension of recent events slowly ebbing from her shoulders. The French Riviera trip had been a whirlwind of drama – Aunt Beatrice's kidnapping, her cousin, the Earl of Wexford, falsely accused of murdering a supposed Italian princess. Now, as the countryside rolled by, she savoured this moment of respite. The chance to relax with her family and support young Alfie Tanner felt like a welcome balm to her frayed nerves.

Alfie, a stable boy from the Hawthorne family estate in Surrey, had always possessed an affinity with horses. Elizabeth's brother, Lord William Hawthorne, spotting his potential, arranged the boy's move to Rosewood Park to train at the racing stables his good friends Lord Ignatius *Iggy* Fairfax and Lady Georgia owned.

Now Alfie was about to race in the Grand National, the most prestigious horse race in the entire country, and Iggy had insisted they stay at his grand estate and be their guests at the race.

The countryside rolled by, dotted with vibrant daffodils and primroses. Their sunny hues complemented the young, emerald wheat shoots swaying in the breeze. Budding hedgerows and the first hints of foliage on towering oaks framed the landscape, casting a patchwork of soft shadows across the landscape. Delicate wildflowers – bluebells, wood anemones, and violets – peeked out from the undergrowth, heralding spring's arrival. Elizabeth nestled against the lush burgundy velvet upholstery, drinking in the picturesque scene. Her spirits lifted at the prospect of the week ahead.

The train swayed, and Meli's shoulder brushed against Elizabeth's, drawing a faint smile from her cousin. Meli's gaze flitted between her three travelling companions. "What exactly is a steeplechase?" she asked.

Elizabeth turned to Meli, her face brightening as she explained. "It's a race over a course filled with obstacles – fences, ditches, all manner of challenges the horses and jockeys have to navigate."

"It's not for the faint-hearted," William chimed in, a note of pride in his voice. "It requires tremendous skill and daring ... qualities Alfie has in abundance." He sat up straighter, his enthusiasm evident. "The Grand National is the pinnacle of steeplechase racing. Georgia tells me Alfie's been working tirelessly for months in preparation."

Caroline reached across and gently squeezed her husband's hand. "I've no doubt he'll make us all proud, no matter how he finishes."

Meli's eyes widened, a grin spreading across her face. "It sounds absolutely thrilling!" She leaned in, her toffee-coloured eyes dancing with curiosity. "Are the stories about Lord Fairfax true? Was he really part of the Discovery Expedition with Ernest Shackleton?"

A faint smile tugged at William's lips. "Indeed, it is true." He paused. "Cost him two toes."

"Two toes?" Meli gasped, the sound almost a scandalised trill.

"Frostbite."

Meli's gaze flitted between the others. "Did he ever share any stories about his adventures?"

William's eyes crinkled at the corners as he glanced at Elizabeth and Caroline. "He did, though he always downplayed his role. Said a little hardship was a small price to pay for being part of such monumental discoveries."

Meli leaned back, her expression one of unabashed admiration. "Lord Fairfax is truly remarkable."

Caroline nudged her husband, her tone teasing. "And very dashing."

Meli practically vibrated with anticipation. "I can't wait to meet him and hear more about his adventures when we arrive."

William chuckled. "I'm sure he has many more stories to share. Just wait until you hear about his expeditions in the Amazon."

"The Amazon?" Meli turned to Elizabeth, practically buzzing with excitement. "I think I would have liked to have been an explorer. Can you imagine it? Venturing into uncharted territories, discovering new things and places..." She sighed wistfully. "Although I wouldn't care to lose any toes."

Elizabeth arched an eyebrow, her expression playful. "How ever would you manage to dance the Charleston in your favourite T-straps with only eight toes?" Her hand flew to her chest in a melodramatic flourish. "You might even have to resort to ... dare I say it ... wearing sensible Oxfords."

Meli visibly shuddered, her nose wrinkling in distaste at the very thought.

Caroline's face brightened as she turned to Meli. "He certainly met his match in Georgia, though. She's quite the adventuress herself."

"Really?"

A warm chuckle rumbled in William's chest as he recounted the tale. "Georgia's spirit and daring are certainly a worthy match for Iggy. Why, she once took her brother's place in a horse race when she was barely sixteen, after he'd injured himself just before the start."

"But were girls even allowed to race back then?"

"No, but that didn't stop Georgia. She simply donned her brother's riding clothes and raced under his name." A hint of admiration crept into William's tone as he spoke. "She won the race … but was promptly disqualified once her true identity was revealed."

"Georgia certainly seems to enjoy defying convention," Caroline said with a playful tilt of her head.

"Goodness, she sounds absolutely remarkable." Meli clasped her hands together. "I can't wait to meet her."

Elizabeth nodded, a fond smile playing on her lips. "Then you must prepare to be enchanted, Meli. Lady Georgia Fairfax is indeed a force of nature and quite stunning, to boot."

"And what about now?" Meli asked. "Do they still travel the world seeking adventures on foreign shores?"

William's shoulders sagged slightly. "No ... not since Iggy's accident."

"Accident?" Meli's voice pitched higher. "What accident?"

He drew in a long breath as if steeling himself before continuing. "Several years ago, Iggy caught the motorcar racing bug. The thrill of speed, the roar of engines ... it consumed him."

Meli gripped the edge of her seat, hanging on every word.

"About two years ago, at Brooklands circuit, Iggy attempted to break the land speed record." William's knuckles whitened as he gripped his armrest. "And his motorcar ... it just ... careened out of control. He was lucky to survive."

Caroline reached over, squeezing her husband's hand. "It was touch-and-go for quite some time, but Georgia never left his side for all those months. She refused to let him give up, and Iggy swears to this day that it was Georgia's love that saved him."

"How terribly romantic," Meli murmured.

"Unfortunately, the injuries he suffered meant they could no longer continue with their old lifestyle."

"How sad," Meli said, sorrow lacing her words.

"Not at all. Iggy's philanthropic interests and the estate keep him busy, and Georgia has her horses and her new business venture."

The steam train rumbled into Aintree station, trading lush countryside for elegant Victorian architecture. Stately brick buildings with intricate facades and decorative iron canopies framed the weathered platform.

The locomotive's pistons slowed their chugging to a steady rumble as the train ground to a halt. Its whistle pierced the air with a shrill cry.

Steam billowed from the engine, hissing and creaking as the metal cooled. Passengers spilled onto the platform, their animated chatter mingling with the shuffling of feet and the clatter of luggage.

William rose, squeezing Caroline's shoulder. "I'll fetch a porter for our luggage." He strode towards the exit.

Elizabeth flipped open her rose-gold compact and scrutinised her reflection. She applied a fresh coat of rose-hued lipstick with practiced precision. Satisfied, she snapped the compact shut and tucked it into her clutch. Meli and Caroline gathered their belongings, ready to disembark.

As they stepped onto the bustling platform, William's tall frame came into view. He directed two porters towards a gleaming Rolls-Royce Silver Ghost. The motorcar's dark grey exterior shimmered, its Spirit of Ecstasy hood ornament catching the afternoon light.

The chauffeur, Simmons, approached in his crisp livery. He dipped his head. "Welcome back, Lord and Lady Hawthorne. Pleasant journey from London, I trust?"

William's lips twitched in a faint smile. "Remarkably so. Thank you, Simmons." He gestured to Elizabeth and Meli as they drew near. "My sister, Lady Elizabeth, and our cousin, Miss Meli Diomaros."

"An honour, Lady Elizabeth, Miss Diomaros." Simmons inclined his head. "Journey not too taxing, I hope?"

Elizabeth smiled warmly. "Not at all, Mr Simmons. We're eager to see Rosewood Park. Lady

Caroline has spoken often of the splendid gardens."

"Indeed, my lady. Finest gardens in all Lancashire," he replied, pride evident in his voice.

The group settled into the plush leather seats as the motorcar purred to life, then glided down the winding country lanes.

Gradually, the landscape gave way to pastoral scenes. Emerald fields stretched out on either side, dotted with white and yellow springtime flowers. Budding trees lined the roads, their tender new leaves fluttering in the breeze. Babbling brooks cut through the landscape, their waters sparkling in the afternoon sun.

Simmons navigated the winding path that bisected the Rosewood Park estate, towering oaks and neatly trimmed lawns flanking their route.

Bursts of colour danced between the thinning trees, drawing Meli's gaze like iron filings to a magnet.

Suddenly, the treeline parted, unveiling a sight that stole her breath away.

A lone figure sat atop a magnificent chestnut mare came thundering across the open fields, fiery hair streaming behind her in a wild crimson banner. With each stride, the horse's powerful muscles rippled beneath its glossy coat, hooves pounding the earth in a thunderous rhythm. The woman moved as one with the animal, her body flowing with effortless grace as she subtly shifted her weight, coaxing every ounce of speed from the steed.

There was a wild, carefree abandon to her riding as if she and the horse were a single, unstoppable entity. Meli watched, transfixed, as the pair cleared a low hedgerow, the mare's front hooves barely skimming the top before landing in a spray of dirt.

"Isn't she magnificent?" Meli breathed, her voice hushed with wonder.

Caroline's lips curved in a fond smile. "That, my dear Meli, is Lady Georgia Fairfax. Our hostess."

Chapter Two

THE ROLLS-ROYCE RUMBLED ALONG the gravel drive, its wheels crunching over the gravel. The chestnut mare surged across the open fields beside it, her powerful legs eating up the ground in a blur of motion. With a flick of the reins, Georgia urged the horse into a full gallop, the wind whipping through her wild auburn curls as they raced alongside the elegant motorcar.

Horse and rider moved as one, soaring over a low stone wall. For a heartbeat, they hung suspended in mid-air before touching down in a flurry of soil and gravel. The grand, sprawling manor of Rosewood Park loomed on the horizon, its stately columns and arched windows etching an imposing silhouette against the afternoon sky.

Neck and neck with the Rolls-Royce, Georgia's mare thundered down the winding drive, hooves pounding the gravel. The motorcar's engine roared as Simmons fought to keep pace. In a final burst of speed, the horse surged ahead. Georgia reined in her mount, bringing it to a smooth, controlled stop mere feet from the approaching motorcar.

The Rolls-Royce's brakes squealed as Simmons wrestled for control, gravel spraying beneath the tyres as he brought the motorcar to a halt.

Georgia swung her leg over the saddle, the gravel crunching beneath her boots as she landed. Striding forward, riding crop tucked under her arm, Georgia beamed as her guests disembarked. She enveloped William and Caroline in a warm embrace. "William, darlin'! And, Caroline, you're looking as beautiful as ever."

Her eyes sparkled as she turned to Elizabeth. "Elizabeth, it's so wonderful to see you again."

Finally, her gaze settled on Meli, her smile widening. "Well, hello there! You must be Meli.

Aren't you just darlin'?" Georgia pulled her into a warm hug.

Meli blinked, momentarily overwhelmed. "Lady Fairfax, I–"

"Call me Georgia, honey," she soothed, treating Meli to a dazzling smile. "I just know you and I are going to be the best of friends."

The grand oaken doors of Rosewood Park swung open. Mr Pritchard, the butler, hurried out to greet the new arrivals.

"Welcome back, Lord and Lady Hawthorne." Mr Pritchard bowed slightly. His keen eyes swept over the rest of the party. "Lady Elizabeth, Miss Diomaros, we're pleased you could join us."

Georgia flashed Mr Pritchard a dazzling smile. "Excellent timing as always, Pritchard." She gestured towards the house. "Pritchard and Mrs Langley will see you all to your rooms." She patted the chestnut's neck. "I'll take this little lady back to the stables for her cool down and join you in the drawing room around seven for pre-dinner cocktails."

With a final wave, Georgia led her horse towards the stables as Pritchard ushered the party inside.

Elizabeth shivered as the spring sunshine gave way to the gloomy interior. Dark oak panelling climbed the walls, punctuated by stern portraits of Iggy's ancestors. Antique furnishings, their wood rich with age, lined the edges of the vast space. At the far end, a grand carved staircase swept upwards, its ornate banister disappearing into the gloom above.

Mrs Langley ushered them up the stairs, the thick burgundy runner muffling their footsteps. On the landing, Elizabeth felt the weight of painted gazes following their progress.

"Lord and Lady Hawthorne, your suite," Mrs Langley announced, gesturing to an intricately carved door. She turned to Elizabeth and Meli. "Lady Elizabeth, Miss Diomaros, you'll be just here. You'll share a bathroom with Lord and Lady Hawthorne."

Meli entered, her gaze darting around the room as they crossed the threshold. The same dark oak panels lined the walls, all the way up to the high ceiling with exposed wooden beams. Twin beds, adorned with deep green velvet bedspreads, sat opposite a shared marble-topped washstand. Heavy brocade curtains, drawn back, revealed windows that seemed to admit more shadows than light.

Meli traced the intricate carvings on the dark wood nightstand. "This decor is rather ... dated." Meli glanced at Elizabeth. "I'd hoped for something a bit more modern."

Elizabeth gave her cousin's arm a gentle squeeze. "Perhaps not the height of fashion, but I'm sure we'll be quite comfortable here."

"I just can't imagine Georgia being content in a place like this. It's so ... stuffy and outdated."

Elizabeth draped her coat neatly over the foot of one of the twin beds. "I know it's not exactly modern, but there's so much history here. These oak panels have seen generations of Fairfaxes."

"No wonder Lord Fairfax spent most of his life abroad. I think I'd rather be anywhere other than this ... mausoleum." Meli glanced up at Elizabeth. "Surely Georgia would prefer to be off exploring the world than being stuck in the countryside."

Elizabeth perched on the edge of the bed. "Georgia may be spirited, but she's devoted to Iggy. Being by his side during his recovery likely means more to her than any far-flung adventure."

"But surely she misses the thrill and freedom?" Meli's gaze drifted to the window. "I know I would."

"I'm sure Georgia's more concerned with her husband's well-being than trekking through jungles. She's found fulfilment in the racing stables here. Her happiness stems from her love for Iggy, not in spite of it."

The cousins whiled away the afternoon hours arranging their belongings and washing off the dust of travel. With the sun nearing the horizon, they shifted their attention to the evening ahead.

Elizabeth stood before the mirror, adjusting her emerald silk evening gown. The sleeveless dress draped elegantly from her shoulders, cinching at the waist before flowing to the floor. Intricate silver beadwork adorned the bodice, tapering off towards the hips. She pinned a silver clip in her inky-dark hair, its design echoing the gown's embellishments.

Meli spun beside her, the champagne-coloured dress shimmering. Layers of crystal-beaded fringe caught the light, sparkling as they swirled at her knees. She struck a pose, one hand on her hip, toffee eyes bright with excitement.

Elizabeth's lips quirked into a smile at her cousin's display. "You look utterly enchanting, Meli."

Meli twirled closer, her smile widening. "And you, Elizabeth, look positively divine."

Her lips twitched, fighting a smile. "And you're positively incorrigible."

Elizabeth swiped rose-pink lipstick across her lips and scrutinised her reflection. Satisfied, she tucked the tube inside her beaded evening bag and grabbed her wrap. "Ready?"

Meli draped a gossamer wrap over her shoulders and snatched up her clutch. "As I'll ever be."

Elizabeth and Meli descended the staircase, the painted eyes of Iggy's ancestors tracking their every move. They entered the Drawing Room, where history seeped from every corner.

A solitary chandelier hung from the high ceiling, its light bolstered by strategically placed brass lamps. Their combined efforts barely illuminated the moss-green velvet sofas and armchairs. Exposed wooden beams crossed overhead, while a faded Oriental rug sprawled across the floor, its once-vibrant patterns dulled by time.

Bookcases dominated one wall, a grand piano commanded a corner, and heavy gold and green drapes concealed the windows, seeming to shrink the room.

Iggy emerged from the fireside, his walking stick striking the floorboards as he approached. Silver hair framed his tanned face, evidence of the two decades between him and Georgia. Yet his blue eyes sparkled with the same charm that had won his young wife's heart.

"My dear Elizabeth, forgive my earlier absence," he said, his rich voice belying the stiffness in his posture. "Magistrate's business in Liverpool ran late. I've only just returned."

Despite his left arm hanging close to his body, Iggy cut an impressive figure in his evening attire. His broad shoulders and athletic frame, though tempered by time and injury, still hinted at the dashing adventurer he'd once been.

Iggy's gaze shifted to Meli. "Ah, and this must be Meli. William spoke of your recent ... involvement in that grim business on the Riviera." His expression sobered as he turned back to Elizabeth. "It seems you've both developed quite a knack for unravelling mysteries."

"Lord Fairfax," Meli began, her voice uncharacteristically hesitant. "It's an honour to–"

"Please, call me Iggy," he interjected, his smile warm despite the gravity of the topic.

"Iggy," Meli repeated, her usual confidence slowly resurfacing as she met his gaze.

Elizabeth observed the exchange, noting the rare sight of her typically effervescent cousin momentarily at a loss for words.

Iggy's gaze drifted to a couple near the fireplace. "Let me introduce you to some of our guests."

A silver-haired man rose with a slight grimace, his wife following suit. As they approached,

Iggy's face lit up with the warmth of old friendship.

"Elizabeth, Meli, allow me to introduce Cecil Bentley, my oldest friend and neighbour, and his wife, Dolores," Iggy said, his hand resting briefly on Cecil's shoulder.

Cecil's eyes crinkled at the corners. "Oldest in every sense, eh, Iggy?" He turned to Elizabeth and Meli, his handshake firm. "A pleasure to meet you both."

Dolores, a plump woman with an elegant steel-grey chignon, smiled warmly. "We've heard so much about you Lady Elizabeth, from Georgia. It's lovely to finally put a face to the name. And Meli, such a pretty name. Greek, unless I'm very much mistaken?"

Meli's eyebrows shot up. "That's right. It's short for Melina. How did you know?"

"Cecil and I have been fortunate enough to visit Greece several times." Dolores's face brightened at the memory. "We fell in love with the country, the people, and of course, the language. Though I'm afraid my pronunciation leaves much to be desired."

Iggy leaned in, a mischievous glint in his eye. "Don't let her fool you. Dolores is quite the linguist."

"Hardly." Dolores waved a dismissive hand, though the corners of her mouth twitched upwards. "Cecil can speak it far better than I."

"Only the important stuff, eh, Cecil?" Iggy nudged his old friend. "Like ordering a large brandy."

Cecil's shoulders shook with silent laughter. "You know me too well, old boy."

Elizabeth watched the easy banter, noting how Iggy and Cecil fell into a familiar rhythm, their shared history evident in every exchanged glance and half-finished sentence. Yet she couldn't help but notice how Iggy seemed to have retained a vitality that time had slowly leached from his old friend.

Elizabeth's attention shifted to the fireplace. William stood with a tall, handsome man, valiantly attempting to draw him into conversation. Despite William's best efforts, his companion's responses were curt, his expression sullen. The man's eyes kept darting towards the nearby settee, his frown deepening with each glance.

Following his gaze, Elizabeth saw Caroline seated beside a woman whose flushed cheeks and loud laughter betrayed her intoxication. Caroline's smile remained fixed, but Elizabeth noticed how her sister-in-law's fingers gripped her glass a little too tightly, betraying her discomfort.

The inebriated woman's voice suddenly cut through the room. "Iggy, darling! Will Georgia be gracing us with her presence tonight?"

Cecil and Dolores stiffened, exchanging a look of barely concealed embarrassment.

Iggy, however, responded smoothly, his tone light. "You know Georgia, always one for a grand entrance."

"Always has to be the centre of attention, you mean," the woman muttered, her words slurring together and carrying further than she likely intended.

Dolores leaned towards Iggy, murmuring, "I'm so sorry. We shouldn't have–"

Iggy patted her hand, his reassuring smile never faltering.

Confusion flickered across Elizabeth's face as she sensed the underlying tension. She glanced at Meli, who raised an eyebrow in silent question.

Iggy cleared his throat. "Elizabeth, Meli, allow me to introduce Mr Dominic Archer," – he nodded towards the sullen man by the fireplace – "and Miss Amelia Stanford." He gestured to the woman beside Caroline.

As Elizabeth's gaze flicked between Dominic and Amelia, she couldn't shake the feeling that she'd stumbled into the middle of some unfinished business.

The drawing room doors swung open, and Georgia swept in, her teal Chanel gown a shimmering cascade of silk and intricate beadwork. Her auburn curls, artfully pinned, framed her face, highlighting her high cheekbones and sparkling eyes.

"I do hope I haven't kept you all waiting," she said, making a beeline for her husband.

Iggy's face softened, his eyes filled with undisguised adoration as he placed a kiss on his wife's cheek. "Not at all, darling. You look absolutely breathtaking, as always."

Amelia's gaze raked over Georgia, her smile sharp as cut glass. "Georgia, darling, finally. I was about to suggest we saddle up and search the paddock for you."

Dolores inhaled sharply, her lips pressing into a thin line as she set her glass down with a little too much force.

Iggy turned to Georgia. "Darling, I don't believe you know Amelia's friend, Mr Dominic Archer."

Dominic stepped forward, took Georgia's hand, and pressed his lips to her knuckles, his gaze lingering on her face. "Lady Fairfax, it's an absolute pleasure."

"Another new friend, Amelia? You're amassing quite a stable." Georgia's tone was light, but her eyes held a challenge.

Amelia's cheeks flushed, though whether from alcohol or irritation, it was impossible to tell. "Speaking of friends, I hope you don't mind, but I've invited someone to join us … a mutual acquaintance."

"Amelia, you told me you'd already spoken to Georgia about your uninvited guest," Dolores snapped.

Amelia's hand fluttered dismissively. "Oh, Georgia and Iggy are far too hospitable to mind one extra guest. And since Reggie is such a good friend of Georgia's, I knew she'd be delighted to see him again."

A shadow flickered across Georgia's face, vanishing before Elizabeth could decipher its meaning. In the blink of an eye, Georgia's composure snapped back into place, her smile unwavering.

"Of course not, Amelia," Georgia purred, her voice smooth as silk. "The more the merrier."

Chapter Three

A DISCREET KNOCK PRECEDED Pritchard's arrival. "Pardon the interruption, Lady Fairfax, but Mr Black has arrived."

Georgia's smile faltered, a flicker of unease flashing across her features before she quickly schooled her expression. She lifted her chin, pasting on a bright, if slightly brittle, smile. "Show him in, Pritchard."

The easy chatter dwindled to a hush as Reggie Black charged into the room with all the pomp and arrogance of a matador entering the bullring. He paused at the epicentre, his dark eyes sweeping over the gathering with a predatory gleam as he raked a hand through his tousled hair, revelling in the attention. The smirk playing at the corners of his mouth widened as he savoured the disruption his arrival had caused.

Georgia faltered for the briefest moment before recovering. "Mr Black, so glad you could join us."

"Always a pleasure, Georgie," he purred, leaning in to press a kiss to each of her cheeks.

Elizabeth caught the brief recoil in Georgia's posture, her unease impossible to hide.

Iggy cut across the room to Georgia's side, a fresh champagne flute in hand. "Darling," he murmured, his fingers brushing hers as he passed her the glass. He angled himself between her and Reggie, his knuckles whitening as he gripped the top of his cane. "Black," he said, his tone measured, "I don't believe you've met everyone." He gestured towards the Hawthornes. "William, Caroline, may I present Mr Reggie Black." Iggy's hand settled on Georgia's waist, a quiet reassurance. "Mr Black, Lord William Hawthorne and his wife, Lady Caroline."

Elizabeth watched as Reggie swooped down on Caroline's hand, his lips lingering a moment too long on her knuckles. Caroline's eyebrow arched slightly, her gaze flicking to Elizabeth in a silent exchange of amused disbelief. Reggie then turned to William, pumping his hand with excessive vigour.

"Lord Hawthorne!" Reggie's voice carried across the room. "Down for the big race on Saturday, I assume?"

William withdrew his hand from Reggie's grip, discreetly flexing his fingers. "Yes, a young lad from our estate is racing. Alfie Tanner."

Reggie's face twisted into a sneer. "You should have saved yourself the trip. Old Tommy's lost his marbles, putting that kid in the National."

Meli bristled, her fingers tightening around her champagne flute. "Kid?" she shot back, her voice sharp. "Alfie's seventeen."

Reggie's gaze raked over Meli, his lips curling into a wolfish grin. "Steady on there, little lady…"

Elizabeth placed a restraining hand on Meli's arm, her voice honey-smooth. "I suppose every jockey's journey has its dawn and its dusk."

Reggie's smirk faltered for a moment, his eyes narrowing as he regarded Elizabeth. He opened his mouth to speak before Iggy interjected. "Reggie, I don't believe you've met Lady

Elizabeth Hawthorne and her cousin, Miss Meli Diomaros."

"Well, well," Reggie drawled, straightening. "You're a lucky man, Hawthorne." His gaze swept over the women, lingering inappropriately. "Surrounded by such ... beautiful ladies."

William stepped forward, his jaw tightening. The warmth in his eyes had cooled to ice. "Perhaps we should stick to discussing the upcoming race, Mr Black," he said, his voice low and controlled.

Amelia swept across the room, her crimson gown hugging her curves and flirting with scandal. The plunging neckline teased, while a daring slit flashed glimpses of her shapely legs with each step.

Reggie greeted Amelia with a roguish grin, took her hand, and brushed his lips against her knuckles. "Amelia, looking as ravishing as always."

Her kohl-rimmed eyes locked onto Reggie. She pressed her lips to his cheek, leaving behind a bold carmine mark. "You're late. I was beginning to think you'd stood me up," she murmured, her thumb sweeping over the smudge.

Reggie's lips quirked into a half-smile. "Had to see a man about a dog." He shrugged, the gesture lazy, almost careless. "You know how it is?"

Amelia's smile faltered, tension tightening her features. "I'm sure you did." Her words slipped out, low and sharp.

Dominic observed the exchange from across the room, his polished veneer fracturing. He swirled the whisky in his glass, eyes glacial as they fixed on Reggie's hand on the small of Amelia's back.

Meli leaned close to Elizabeth, her breath warm against her cousin's ear. "I thought Mr Archer was Miss Stanford's boyfriend."

Elizabeth's gaze darted between Dominic and the couple. She inclined her head towards the seething man, her voice low. "So, it seems, did Mr Archer."

The sharp clink of Dominic's glass hitting the table drew curious glances. His smile, a slash across his face, held a dangerous edge. His gaze, unwavering from Reggie and Amelia, spoke of a predator sizing up its prey. The muscles in his jaw pulsed as he took a measured step forward, the air around him crackling with quiet menace.

Guests shifted uncomfortably, their laughter too loud, their smiles too bright as all eyes darted between Dominic and the oblivious couple.

Just as Dominic's foot lifted for another step, Pritchard materialised at the doorway. "Pardon the intrusion, Lady Fairfax, but dinner is served."

The collective sigh of relief was almost audible. Guests hurried towards the dining room, grateful for the timely interruption. Dominic froze mid-stride, his face a mask of barely contained fury. He inhaled sharply, fingers flexing at his sides, before forcing a brittle smile and following the others. His eyes, however, never left Reggie's back as they filed out of the room.

Georgia and Iggy ushered their guests into the dining room. The space exuded the same sombre, antiquated air, much like the rest of the house. Its dark wood panelling absorbed much of the light from the imposing Gothic chandelier overhead.

Amelia hips swayed with feline charm as she sashayed towards the dining table. "Since your seating plan is already askew, we simply must squeeze Reggie in next to me."

Elizabeth caught Georgia's narrowed gaze and heard her mutter, "And whose fault is that?"

Georgia quickly composed herself and announced with forced brightness, "Of course, everyone, please sit ... wherever you like."

As the guests settled, Elizabeth watched Amelia steal a quick glance at Dominic from beneath her lowered lashes. Her hand lingered on Reggie's arm as she laughed, the sound a touch too loud. Dominic's jaw clenched, his eyes never leaving the pair. The earlier tension, briefly dispelled by the change of setting, began to seep back in.

She angled her head towards Dominic, attempting to break the awkward silence. "I hear Mr Black is the favourite for Saturday's race. He's certainly gained quite a following, if the newspapers are to be believed."

Dominic's hand hovered over his soup spoon. "Reggie Black certainly has a knack for winning, but his methods are ... shall we say ... questionable."

She paused, her own spoon halfway to her lips. "Questionable? How do you mean?"

"Let's just say Mr Black isn't a man to play by the rules and his choice of associates leaves much to be desired."

"Ah, I see." Elizabeth's gaze flicked between Dominic and the couple across the table, whispering and laughing as if they hadn't a care in the world. "And I imagine that doesn't sit well with you, given your ... connection with Miss Stanford. His attentions towards her must be something of a concern."

She pondered Dominic's words, her gaze drifting to Amelia and Reggie. Amelia revelled in Reggie's attention, her flirtation brazen and unabashed despite Dominic's presence across the table. Her casual disregard for propriety spoke volumes.

With the Grand National looming, Reggie was undeniably the man of the moment, the focus of every conversation. And Amelia, it seemed, was more than happy to bask in the reflected limelight of his fame.

Her eyes shifted to the other end of the table, where William, Caroline, and Meli sat with Iggy.

Though their voices were low, she could sense the underlying discomfort. William's usually impeccable posture had calcified, his knuckles bloodless around his wine glass. Caroline's smile, though present, never reached her eyes, a flicker of strain marring her composure. Meli, typically effervescent, now fidgeted with her napkin, her gaze darting between her cousins as if seeking reassurance. Even Iggy's usual affability seemed to have deserted him, a muscle in his cheek twitching as he side-eyed the couple.

The air hung heavy with unspoken tension, a brittle veneer of politeness threatening to crack at any moment.

Dominic jumped to his feet, the legs of his chair scraping harshly against the floorboards. Heads whipped around, startled by the suddenness of his movement. Without sparing anyone a glance, he threw his napkin onto the table.

"I need some air," he muttered, his voice tight, before turning on his heel and striding towards the door.

Elizabeth's eyes followed him, but it was Amelia's reaction that caught her attention. Amelia's gaze was locked on Dominic's back as he left the room, her focus entirely on him, not Reggie. The door slammed shut behind him.

Amelia blinked, her gaze flicking back to Reggie, but the ease in her smile seemed forced now, her flirtation less animated than before.

As the door slammed behind Dominic, Amelia's laughter broke the brief silence, louder than before, yet hollow. Her flirtation with Reggie continued, but it had lost its earlier zeal – her gestures were more restrained, her gaze occasionally drifting back to the door. Reggie, oblivious to the change, carried on with his usual swagger, while across the table, Dolores Bentley leaned towards Georgia, her whisper too pointed to be fully private but just quiet enough for discretion.

"Oh, Georgia, I'm so sorry. We should have left Amelia at home. She's been impossible all week. I know one shouldn't speak ill of one's family … but I'll be glad when she returns to London." Dolores's fingers tightened around her wine glass.

Georgia's eyes flicked towards Amelia before returning to Dolores. "These things happen. It's hardly your fault."

"But one can't help but feel responsible. We've tried our best since her parents passed, we really have, but Amelia's always been so…"

"Headstrong," Cecil supplied, his gaze fixed on his plate. "It's like we've always said, money's never a good substitute for attention, especially where children are concerned."

Dolores pursed her lips. "She's her own worst enemy. Always chasing the next thrill, and with her wealth…"

"There's precious little out of reach," Cecil finished, subtly signalling to a nearby footman for a refill.

Georgia leaned in slightly towards Dolores. "Is it serious between them – Amelia and Mr Archer?"

Dolores shifted in her seat, casting a quick glance at Amelia before turning back to Georgia. "With Amelia, it's hard to say. But he's lasted longer than most."

The last of the dessert plates disappeared from the table, seemingly of their own accord

– the footmen's movements so practiced and unobtrusive they barely registered.

Amelia's laughter pierced the stilted conversation once more, but Elizabeth noticed her eyes darting to the door Dominic had stormed through earlier. On the surface, Amelia seemed to have it all – beauty, wealth, and men vying for her attention. Yet, as Elizabeth observed the heiress's forced gaiety and restless glances, she couldn't help but wonder if all that glittered in Amelia's world was nothing more than a lonely, gilded cage.

An undercurrent of tension followed the party as they migrated back to the drawing room. Elizabeth's gaze was drawn to Dominic the moment they entered. His white-knuckled grip on the almost empty tumbler betrayed his barely contained fury.

"Georgia dear, might we take our leave?" Dolores asked, pressing her fingers to her temple. "This headache…" Her eyes darted pointedly towards Amelia, who giggled at Reggie's whispered words.

Iggy followed Dolores's gaze and nodded. "Of course. I'll have Simmons bring the car around. Quicker than summoning your own chauffeur."

Glass met marble with a sharp clink as Dominic set down his tumbler. "I think it's time we left as well, Amelia."

"But I'm having such a lovely evening."

Iggy cleared his throat. "We were actually thinking of calling it a night. Our guests must be ready to retire after such a long journey."

"But I want to stay," she protested, her lower lip jutting out like a pouting child.

Reggie's grin widened, flicking a quick glance at Dominic. "How about we carry on at Adelina's? What do you say?"

Amelia's eyes sparkled with excitement. "Oh, yes, I adore Adelina's!"

Dominic's voice lowered, a hint of steel beneath the calm. "Enough with this nonsense," he snapped. "We're leaving now."

Reggie's lips twitched as he straightened his shoulders. "Surely that's Amelia's decision?"

Elizabeth watched as Amelia's gaze danced between the two men, satisfaction glinting in her eyes.

Dominic rounded on Reggie, brow furrowed and fists clenching. "This doesn't concern you, Black. Stay out of it."

"Or what?" Reggie stepped closer.

William surged forward, attempting to come between them. "Gentlemen, this isn't–"

Dominic's fist shot out, striking Reggie square in the jaw.

Gasps erupted as Reggie reeled backwards, his head smashing against the side table before he crashed to the floor with a sickening thud.

Chapter Four

Meli jabbed the last pin into her dark curls, securing them into a stylish faux bob. She spun away from the mirror, her cream-coloured day dress swishing around her legs. "I can't believe the way Mr Black and Miss Stanford behaved last night. And in front of everyone. No wonder Mr Archer punched him on the nose."

Elizabeth fastened the last pearl button on her emerald green day dress. "Thank goodness William and Mr Bentley intervened or heaven knows what might have happened."

"Well, I think Mr Black deserved it," Meli declared, planting her hands on her hips. "And did you see the look on Miss Stanford's face? She seemed to positively revel in all the drama."

Elizabeth rose from the bed, smoothing out the lace at her cuffs. "I'm not sure anyone came out of that situation looking particularly admirable. I do hope it doesn't dampen the mood for the entire weekend."

Meli scoffed, her toffee-coloured eyes darting around the room. "If anything's going to dampen the mood, it's this dreary, old mausoleum. Even on such a bright spring morning, it feels as though we've been transported back to the dark ages."

"Oh, Meli." Elizabeth chuckled, shaking her head. "Not everyone craves the latest fashions as you do. Some people find comfort in tradition."

Meli shook her head as she slipped into her T-strap heels. "You know, when I first met Iggy, I thought, 'Goodness, he's ancient!' But then he started telling his stories, and suddenly he was as dashing as any romantic hero from a novel."

Elizabeth reached for her wide-brimmed hat and carefully secured it atop her neatly coiffed hair. A faint smile played on her lips. "Iggy certainly has a way of captivating an audience."

"You know, I can't help feeling a little sorry for Miss Stanford."

Elizabeth glanced up, adjusting her hat in the mirror. "How so?"

"Well, with all that money, how can she ever be truly confident someone likes her for herself? At least Iggy doesn't have that problem with Georgia." She bit her lip, hesitating. "Do you think Mr Archer is only with Miss Stanford for her fortune?"

"It's difficult to say. Not many men would tolerate last night's antics, but whether his inclinations are romantic or financial, it's difficult to tell." She sighed, meeting Meli's gaze in the mirror. "Some have a talent for masking their true selves and motivations, that it's impossible to tell where truth ends and the lie begins."

Elizabeth stole a quick glance at the clock. "We need to hurry."

"Oh my, you're right. We don't want to be late." Meli gathered her belongings while Elizabeth slipped on her gloves.

They made their way downstairs to find Georgia and Caroline waiting in the entrance hall.

"Would you look at you two." Georgia's voice carried a teasing edge, hands firmly planted on her hips. "Aren't you a sight for sore eyes?"

Meli, with a twinkle in her eye, dropped into an exaggerated curtsey. "Why, thank you, Lady Fairfax," she quipped, flashing a playful grin.

Georgia chuckled, shaking her head. "How about we get this show on the road, ladies?"

Outside, Georgia's ivory Vauxhall 30-98 sat waiting in the driveway.

Caroline's gaze lingered on the driver's seat, her brow furrowing slightly. "Won't Simmons be driving us?"

"Not today," Georgia replied, patting the car's bonnet. "I'll be your chauffeur."

"How thrilling!" Meli clasped her hands together.

Georgia turned to her. "How'd you like to ride up front with me, darlin'?"

"Oh, I'd love to!" Meli said, her smile widening.

Elizabeth slid into the back seat beside Caroline. Her sister-in-law's fingers gripped the edge of her seat. Elizabeth caught Caroline's eye, offering a reassuring smile. If Georgia handled a motorcar with the same gusto she displayed in the saddle, they were in for quite a ride.

Georgia released the clutch, and the Vauxhall lurched forward. The countryside flew past in a whirl of green fields and flowering hedgerows as she navigated the winding lanes with the same confidence she displayed on horseback.

Elizabeth glanced at her sister-in-law. Caroline sat rigid, her eyes firmly shut, lips moving in silent prayer. In contrast, Meli leaned forward in her seat, drinking in the scenery with wide-eyed wonder.

"This is absolutely exhilarating!" Meli called over the rush of wind, her curls escaping their pins.

As the Vauxhall roared along the country roads, Elizabeth contemplated how Iggy's accident had reshaped his and Georgia's adventurous life. To casual observers, Lady Fairfax seemed at peace with her new normal. Yet Elizabeth couldn't help but wonder – could Georgia, a woman who once chased thrills across continents, truly find fulfilment in the tamer pursuits of horseback rides and motorcar jaunts?

As the ivory Vauxhall swept through the wrought-iron gates, the Aintree Gentlemen's Club came into view. The imposing Edwardian building of red brick and ivy stood proudly, its arched windows and entrance exuding an air of exclusivity.

Georgia brought the motorcar to a halt and handed the keys to a waiting valet in a smart navy uniform. "Thank you," she said with a warm smile. She linked her arm through Meli's and led the way towards the heavy oak doors.

The entrance hall greeted them with dark wood panelling and gleaming floors. Portraits of stern-faced gentlemen lined the walls, their painted eyes seeming to appraise the new-comers. A grand staircase curved upwards, its balustrade intricately carved.

Georgia moved through the hall confidently, nodding to several elegantly dressed ladies as she passed. "Ladies, how lovely to see you," she said, her voice carrying across the room. She gestured to her companions. "May I introduce my dear friends – Lady Caroline Hawthorne, her sister-in-law, Lady Elizabeth, and Miss Meli Diomaros."

Dolores Bentley's hand fluttered in the air, catching Georgia's eye from across the dining room. "Thank goodness you're here," she said, nodding towards her companion. Exasperation laced her words.

Amelia slumped in her chair, gripping a crystal tumbler, her bloodshot eyes barely open. She brought the glass to her lips, grimacing as the thick tomato concoction hit her tongue. A shudder ran through her, and she lowered the glass after barely a sip.

Elizabeth and her companions took their seats at the table, while a footman hovered nearby, a tray of champagne flutes at the ready. She waved hers away with a polite smile, her attention drawn to Amelia, memories of the previous evening flooding back.

Amelia's laughter had rung out, growing louder with every glass of champagne she consumed. She'd draped herself over Mr Black, her fingers trailing down his arm as Mr Archer looked on. The evening ended prematurely with Dominic's fist connecting with Reggie's jaw, sending him crashing to the floor.

Amelia slouched into her chair, her unfocused gaze fixed on some distant point. Beside her, Dolores's eyes darted from table to table, her mouth tightening with each glance. She shifted closer to Amelia, her whisper sharp. "Sit up straight, for goodness' sake. People are staring."

Amelia's shoulders twitched upwards, a half-hearted attempt at sitting straight. "Happy now?" she grumbled, her voice rough. She lifted her glass, grimacing as she forced down another sip of the red mixture.

Dolores's lips pressed into a bloodless line, a soft 'tsk' escaping as she turned away.

Elizabeth cleared her throat, keen to break the tension. "And what of Mr Bentley and Mr Archer? What are their plans for this afternoon? Will they be joining you later?"

At the mention of Dominic, Amelia's hand jerked, red liquid sloshing dangerously close to the crystal's rim. Wincing, she waved her free hand dismissively. "Dominic's most likely sulking," she muttered. "I'll buy him some new cufflinks or perhaps a watch. That usually brightens his mood."

Elizabeth's gaze found Meli's, the truth unspoken but understood. Perhaps the nature of Miss Stanford and Mr Archer's relationship was indeed more transactional than tender.

Elizabeth's gaze swept across the dining room. Nearby patrons exchanged furtive glances, their whispers barely concealed behind raised hands.

"It's such a lovely afternoon. Perhaps we could continue our luncheon on the balcony?"

Dolores's eyes darted to a table where two women quickly averted their stares. She turned back to Elizabeth, a grateful smile playing at her lips.

Caroline's eyes met Elizabeth's, a flash of understanding passing between them. "An excellent suggestion. Some fresh air would be most welcome."

Georgia raised her hand, catching a passing footman's attention. She rose from her chair. "We're finding it a little ... stuffy in here. Please arrange for our luncheon to be served on the balcony."

They followed Georgia out onto the balcony, exchanging the dining room's suffocating air of propriety for the warmth of the spring afternoon. They chose a table with a clear view of Aintree racecourse, its emerald expanse unfurling before them.

The famous track wound through the landscape, each bend and straight promising the thrill of glory or the sting of defeat in the upcoming Grand National.

The fresh air seemed to lift the mood. Even Amelia brightened as the waiter arrived with the first course.

Georgia squinted, leaning over the balustrade. She rose to her feet, shielding her eyes from the sun. "I think that's Tommy and young Alfie down there. Looks like they're inspecting the course for the big race."

Amelia's head snapped up, her eyes darting across the green expanse. "Reggie!" she shrieked, half-rising from her chair.

Dolores's fingers dug into Amelia's arm, tugging her back down. "Amelia, please," she hissed through clenched teeth, her cheeks flushing crimson. She cast apologetic glances at nearby tables, where other patrons had paused mid-conversation to stare.

Undeterred, Amelia shook off Dolores's grip and waved wildly. "Over here, darling!"

Reggie's head tilted up. With a dramatic flourish, he pressed his fingers to his lips and blew an exaggerated kiss skyward.

Dolores slumped in her chair, one hand covering her eyes

Tommy joined a cluster of men near the rails, his animated gestures punctuating his conversation. Alfie hovered on the periphery, hands buried in his pockets, his gaze fixed on the ground as he scuffed at the turf with the toe of his boot.

"Poor Alfie." Caroline sighed. "He looks so ... out of place."

Georgia's eyes softened as she watched the young jockey. "He's the new kid in town. It'll take time before he's accepted. But Tommy will take care of him."

Reggie cut across the field, making his way towards Alfie. He halted inches from the younger man, his lips moving rapidly. Alfie's shoulders hunched, his body twisting away from Reggie.

Reggie's hand shot out, his finger connecting with Alfie's shoulder. Alfie pivoted, taking quick steps in the opposite direction, but Reggie kept pace.

"Oi, kid!" Reggie's shout carried across the field. His hand clamped down on Alfie's arm, spinning him around.

Meli sucked in a sharp breath, her body tensing. "Someone needs to stop him."

Reggie's finger jabbed at Alfie's chest. Alfie's hand flew up, batting it away as he straightened to his full height.

Tommy's head snapped up, his conversation forgotten. Men converged from all directions, their hurried steps kicking up small clouds of dust.

As Reggie cocked his fist, Tommy thrust himself between the jockeys, his arms spread wide. Two men materialised behind Reggie, each grasping an arm and hauling him backwards. Tommy's mouth moved rapidly, his gaze locked on Reggie before he turned, steering Alfie away with a hand on his shoulder.

Meli's gaze trailed after Alfie's retreating form. "Do you really think he has a chance at the Grand National?"

A harsh laugh escaped Amelia's lips. "Against Reggie? Not a hope in Hades."

Dolores's eyes narrowed. "Amelia," she hissed, her tone sharp.

Amelia's shoulder rose in a careless shrug as she raised her champagne flute. "What? It's the truth. Unless Reggie Black drops dead mid-race, that boy doesn't stand a chance."

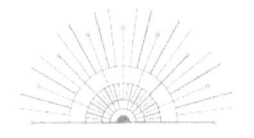

Chapter Five

THE DAMP GRASS SQUELCHED underfoot as Elizabeth and Meli crossed the grounds of Rosewood Park. The sky hung low and grey, hinting at the possibility of rain later in the day.

As they neared the stables, the familiar scent of hay and horses filled the air, mingling with the sharp tang of leather. The sounds of grooms at work and horses shifting restlessly reached them, a reminder of the preparations for the upcoming race.

"I do hope Alfie's in better spirits today. That dreadful Mr Black was simply beastly to him at the club yesterday."

"William mentioned Alfie seemed out of sorts last night." Elizabeth's gaze swept over the bustling figures ahead, her thoughts circling back to yesterday's exchange between Alfie and Reggie. The memory of Reggie's behaviour still left a bitter taste. "I'm sure he'll appreciate seeing some friendly faces."

Elizabeth scanned the stable yard, her eyes flitting from horse to groom. The air hummed with activity – the swish of brushes, the clink of metal, the occasional snort of a horse. She paused, spotting a familiar figure.

Elizabeth nudged Meli with her elbow and inclined her head towards the far end of the yard. "There's Alfie."

The young jockey worked methodically, his brush gliding over the coat of a chestnut mare. His brow relaxed, the hint of a smile playing at the corners of his mouth.

Meli moved to step forward. Elizabeth's hand shot out, gripping her cousin's wrist.

"Hold on." Her gaze had caught on something beyond Alfie.

Meli followed her line of sight, sucking in a sharp breath. Reggie Black had appeared, swaggering between the stalls. His usual smirk clashed with the purple bruise blooming around his eye.

Without a word, the cousins ducked behind a nearby stable door.

Elizabeth and Meli peered from behind the stable door as Reggie's gaze swept over Alfie. The corner of his mouth twitched upwards, eyes glinting with malice. "Shouldn't you be off somewhere, mucking out stalls?"

Alfie's hand froze mid-stroke, the brush hovering over the mare's coat. His shoulders stiffened, knuckles whitening around the brush handle. His face remained still, but a vein pulsed at his temple.

Reggie stepped closer, his voice dropping to a stage whisper. "I suppose that's what happens when you let a woman run things. Living out here in the middle of nowhere with that cripple of a husband of hers has made her lose her mind. I mean, what was she thinking putting a kid in the National?"

Alfie's jaw clenched, a muscle jumping beneath his skin. His eyes, fixed on the horse's flank, narrowed to slits. "You watch your mouth, Black," he said, each word clipped and hard. "Don't you dare talk about Lady Fairfax like that."

Reggie threw his head back and laughed, the sound sharp and mocking. "Lady Fairfax? Trust me, boy, she's no lady. And I'll say what I damn well please."

The stable door groaned beneath Elizabeth's grip.

"Leave the boy alone." Tommy strode into view, his boots kicking up small clouds of dust. The lines on his face deepened as he scowled at Reggie.

A second figure shuffled in Tommy's wake. The man's shirt clung to his damp skin, dark patches spreading under his arms. He dabbed at his forehead with a crumpled handkerchief, his eyes darting between Alfie and Reggie.

Reggie's mouth snapped shut, his smirk faltering. He pivoted to face the newcomers, his bruised eye now fully visible.

Alfie's fingers uncurled from the brush, one by one. His chest rose and fell in measured breaths.

Elizabeth pressed closer to the gap in the door.

Reggie's gaze slid to the pasty-faced man. "What's the matter, Doc? Not had your morning fix yet?"

Dr Franklin's eyes darted between the others. His hand crept to his collar and tugged at it as if it were suddenly too tight.

Tommy stepped forward, arms folding across his chest. His eyes narrowed to slits. "Get out of here, Black, before I throw you out myself."

A smirk tugged at the corners of Reggie's mouth. "Steady on there, Tommy, old man. You wouldn't want to give yourself a heart attack now, would you?"

Reggie's gaze swept over Alfie once more. His upper lip curled. "A word of advice, kid. Fancy silks won't hide the stench of a stable rat forever."

Colour flooded Alfie's face, his hands balling into fists at his sides. He surged forward, but Tommy's arm shot out, a solid barrier across his chest.

"Easy, lad," Tommy murmured, each word clipped and low. Alfie's chest heaved as he glared at Reggie's retreating back, but he remained rooted to the spot.

Tommy's gaze flicked to Dr Franklin. He cleared his throat. "Doc, got a moment? Starlight's not right."

Dr Franklin flinched. His eyes darted between Tommy and the stable exit. He shifted his weight from foot to foot. "I … well, I suppose I could spare a few minutes."

Tommy nodded and turned on his heel. Dr Franklin trailed behind, his footsteps unsteady.

Starlight's ears flicked back and forth as they approached her stall. The mare pawed at the ground, nostrils flaring.

Dr Franklin edged closer, his movements stiff and disjointed. His hands skimmed over Starlight's leg, a slight tremor visible in his fingers.

The vet reached for his bag. The clasp slipped through his fingers once, twice. A small vial tumbled from the open bag, and shattered on the stable floor.

Dr Franklin crouched, fingers scrabbling at the shards. "Reggie was right. I should have had that morning fix … of coffee."

His hands trembled as he thrust the remaining vials at Tommy. "Perhaps you'd better do it.

Keep an eye on her. If there's any change, let me know immediately."

Dr Franklin straightened, brushing at his knees. His gaze flitted around the stable as he packed away his equipment, movements jerky and uncertain. "I'll, uh, I'll check back this afternoon. Just to be sure."

Tommy's face remained impassive. "Right, Doc. We'll keep a close watch."

Dr Franklin's steps were measured but hurried as he made his way out of the stable. Tommy turned his attention to the syringe, his movements practiced and sure as he administered the injection to Starlight.

Tommy capped the syringe with a soft click then ran his hand over Starlight's flank. Alfie stood by the stall door, shoulders hunched, hands balled into fists at his sides.

"Black's all bluff and bluster. Don't let him get to you, lad."

Alfie's fists unclenched slowly. His chin lifted a fraction, but his gaze remained fixed on the hay-strewn floor.

Tommy's footsteps faded, the sound of his retreat punctuated by the soft nickering of horses. Silence settled over the stable, broken only by Starlight's occasional snort.

The stable door creaked open. Elizabeth winced, freezing mid-step. Meli bumped into her from behind, a muffled "oof" escaping her lips. Alfie's head snapped up, his eyes widening as they emerged from their hiding spot.

Alfie's shoulders straightened as he spotted Elizabeth and Meli. His fingers stilled on the brim of his flat cap, a smile crinkling the corners of his eyes. "Lady Elizabeth. What are you doing here?"

Elizabeth hesitated, Reggie's sneering face flashing in her mind. Should she mention his altercations with Reggie? Ask if he was alright? Her eyes flicked to his face, searching for signs of distress. He seemed well enough, but was he just putting on a brave front? She weighed the options, torn between her desire to offer support and her reluctance to embarrass him. In the end, she decided against it.

"We thought you could use some support," she said, gesturing to Meli. "My cousin, Miss Diomaros."

Alfie dipped his head, the brim of his cap twisting in his fingers as a flush spread across his cheeks. "Miss Diomaros."

The chestnut mare shifted restlessly, her tail flicking against the wooden walls of the stall.

"She's beautiful," Meli murmured, reaching towards the chestnut's velvet muzzle.

Alfie's eyebrows rose. "Careful, miss. She–"

The mare's teeth snapped, barely missing Meli's fingers. She stumbled back with a yelp.

Alfie's lips twitched, his eyes dancing with unspoken amusement.

Elizabeth cleared her throat. "Alfie, about your parents..." Her hand dipped into her pocket. "They wanted to be here, but your father's leg..." She trailed off, producing a small wrapped package.

Alfie's calloused hands cradled the gift. The paper fell away, revealing a leather cord and a misshapen metal charm. His throat worked silently.

"Your father made it for luck. They may not be here, but they're with you in spirit." She gave him a reassuring smile. "And the Hawthornes will be cheering you on."

Alfie's jaw clenched, his eyes fixed on the charm. He swallowed hard, fingers closing around it as he fought to keep his emotions in check.

"Oi, Alfie! Sir Gallant needs grooming before his afternoon exercise!"

Alfie's head snapped up. He tucked the charm carefully into his pocket. "I'd best get on."

Elizabeth touched his arm lightly. "Of course. Best of luck for tomorrow's race."

"We'll be cheering for you."

Alfie's cheeks flushed as he tugged at the brim of his cap. "Thank you, Lady Elizabeth, Miss Diomaros. I'll do my best to make you proud."

Elizabeth's fingers briefly rested on his shoulder. "Just do your best. No one can ask for more."

Leaving Alfie to his work, Elizabeth and Meli exited the stables, halting at the sight of Dr Franklin slumped in the driver's seat of a motorcar, his head lolling backwards.

Elizabeth stepped closer to the car. "Dr Franklin?"

The doctor's eyes flew open, wide and glassy. His fingers scrabbled at his rolled-up sleeve, hastily unfurling it over his forearm.

"Er ... yes," he mumbled, his gaze darting between Elizabeth and Meli. "Just ... resting my eyes. Late night with a mare in foal."

Elizabeth's eyes narrowed as she took in his pallid complexion. "Are you certain you're alright?"

Dr Franklin's mouth twisted into what might have been a smile. His hand trembled as he glanced at his watch. "Perfectly fine. But I'm late for my next appointment. If you'll excuse me..."

As he fumbled with the ignition, Elizabeth leaned closer. "Dr Franklin, there's blood on your sleeve."

His arm jerked back, knocking against the steering wheel. "It's nothing." His voice cracked. "Occupational hazard. Now, if you'll pardon me..."

The engine sputtered to life. Dr Franklin yanked the gearshift and the car lurched forward and away.

Meli's mouth fell open as she watched the motorcar disappear down the drive. "How odd."

Elizabeth's lips pressed into a thin line, her gaze still fixed on the cloud of dust left in Dr Franklin's wake. "Indeed it was, Meli. Indeed it was."

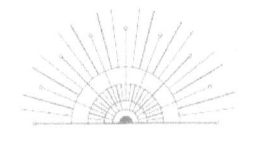

Chapter Six

THE CLOCK STRUCK FOUR as Elizabeth pinned the last strand of her dark bob in place. She smoothed her emerald dress, its embroidered vines subtle against the silk. In the mirror, she caught Meli's reflection, her cousin already dressed in coral chiffon, a string of pearls dangling from her fingers.

Meli twirled before the mirror, her fingers smoothing the silk of her dress. "I wonder if there will be any handsome young men in attendance today," she mused. "Perhaps we'll find some dashing gentlemen who might pique even your interest, Elizabeth."

Elizabeth adjusted her sleeves, a wry smile curving her lips. "I'm sorry to disappoint you, but this afternoon's soiree is more about business than pleasure. Caroline mentioned that Georgia is hoping to find investors for her racing venture."

Meli's eyes widened as a small, involuntary gasp escaped her lips. "But why would they need investors?" She lowered her voice. "You don't think they are in financial straits, do you? That would certainly explain why this house is so old-fashioned and musty."

Elizabeth applied her lipstick with a steady hand, meeting her cousin's reflection in the mirror. "No, not at all. But it seems Georgia wants to prove she can manage it on her own, without relying on Iggy's money."

Relief flooded Meli's features. "I must admit, I do admire Georgia's independent spirit."

Elizabeth's lips quirked upwards. "From what I've heard, she does have a knack for ruffling the old guard's feathers."

"I can't help but wonder," Meli said, adjusting the clasp of her bracelet, "if Miss Stanford will make an appearance. And which of her suitors will she favour? Mr Archer or Mr Black?"

Elizabeth set down her hairbrush on the vanity. "Mr Black wouldn't dare show his face here.

Not after that ugly business with Mr Archer." She reached for her perfume atomiser, her gaze distant. "Miss Stanford, though, seems to wear scandal like a fashion accessory."

Meli swept a vibrant coral across her lips, the hue perfectly matching her dress. "Poor Mrs Bentley," she said, turning to Elizabeth. "She was utterly aghast at Miss Stanford's antics at the track yesterday. I can't fathom what she sees in Mr Black, you know. He may rule the racecourse, but off it, he's an absolute cad."

"I couldn't agree more." Elizabeth grabbed her clutch, her eyes meeting Meli's in the mirror. "Ready?"

"As I'll ever be."

They made their way downstairs, the sound of guests arriving for Georgia's soiree drifting through the open windows. Elizabeth's mind wandered to the morning's events at the stables – Reggie's taunts, Alfie's determination not to let anyone down, Dr Franklin's strange behaviour. She pushed the thoughts aside. For now, at least, they had a party to attend.

"Oh bother, I've forgotten my shawl." Elizabeth halted midway down the staircase, her hand resting on the banister. "You go on ahead, Meli. I'll join you in a moment."

As Meli's coral dress disappeared from view, Elizabeth ascended the stairs. She paused before a portrait, her eyes drawn to the nameplate beneath. The canvas captured a handsome gentleman – Iggy's grandfather – his eyes twinkling with a hint of mischief that seemed to run in the family.

Raised voices drifted across the landing – Iggy's deep rumble and Georgia's unmistakable American accent. Elizabeth paused, her hand still on the banister. She hesitated for a moment, then inched closer to the partially open door of Iggy's study.

"I don't understand this insistence on involving strangers, Georgia," Iggy said, his tone tinged with exasperation. "I've said I'm happy to provide the funds myself."

"But that's just it, Iggy," Georgia retorted, her words sharp with frustration. "I want to do this by myself, without relying on your handouts."

Iggy's response carried a note of disbelief. "Handouts? Darling, you're my wife. I'd rather give you the money than have someone like Enzo Bellini involved."

Georgia's clipped tones cut through the air. "What do you have against him? Enzo's money is as good as anyone's."

"Hardly," Iggy replied, his voice heavy with disapproval. "You know the kind of man he is, the things he's involved in. I can't believe you've invited him here, to our home."

A sharp laugh escaped Georgia. "You just don't get it, do you? Do you think I don't know what people say about me, what they've always said?"

"I don't care about that. Let them talk."

"But I do, and that's why I need to do this myself."

"Then let me give you the money. I can be a silent investor. No one need know."

"I'd know..." Georgia's voice softened momentarily before hardening again. "Look, I don't have time for this. I have guests to attend to."

The sudden scrape of a chair against the floor jolted Elizabeth. Footsteps approached the door, each one louder than the last. Her heart hammered against her ribs as she searched for an escape. The hanging tapestry - her only hope. She slipped behind it, pressing herself against the wall. The heavy fabric scratched her face, its musty odour stinging her nostrils as she held her breath, straining to hear over the rush of blood in her ears.

The footsteps receded, their echo fading into silence. Elizabeth waited a moment longer, her pulse gradually slowing. She eased out from behind the tapestry, wincing as the rough fabric caught on her dress. The odour clung to her as she smoothed her skirt, her mind whirling with questions.

Iggy and Georgia's voices replayed in her head, their usual warmth replaced by an unfamiliar strain. Elizabeth frowned, puzzled by the discord she'd witnessed between the couple who'd always seemed so content. Who was this Enzo Bellini that could cause such tension? And why was Iggy so adamant about keeping him away from Georgia's business venture?

Elizabeth retreated to her bedroom, her mind still churning over the heated exchange she'd overheard. She retrieved her shawl and draped it around her shoulders, then made her way downstairs.

Floral scents enveloped her as she entered the conservatory, her gaze sweeping across the elegant furnishings – wicker chairs and tables and marble floor tiles adorned with art deco-patterned rugs. Ornate glass panels lined the vaulted ceiling, filtering the soft, muted light of the overcast sky. Trailing vines and fragrant flowers lent a sense of tranquillity, a welcome reprieve from both the formal, old-fashioned decor of the rest of the house.

Her eyes drifted across the room, settling on William and Caroline, deep in conversation with the Bentleys. Nearby, Meli seemed to be valiantly attempting to engage a visibly disinterested Amelia Stanford in conversation.

Elizabeth smoothed her features, pushing aside her curiosity about the argument as she moved to join the others.

Amelia turned on her heel the moment Elizabeth arrived, making a beeline for a man who seemed to ooze insincerity. Meli grabbed Elizabeth's elbow, her eyes wide with exasperation. "What took you so long? I was beginning to think

I'd have to feign a fainting spell to invoke some kind of response from Miss Stanford."

Elizabeth's fingers fidgeted with her shawl. "Sorry, I got held up."

Across the room, Amelia's tinkling laughter rose above the general chatter. Meli rolled her eyes. "I console myself that Miss Stanford's lack of interest had more to do with my gender than the calibre of my conversation."

She watched as Amelia leaned in close to her companion, whispering something that set off another round of giggles. "She does seem to have a type, doesn't she?"

Caroline caught Elizabeth's eye, beckoning her and Meli to join their circle. "Elizabeth, Meli, come and join us. Mr and Mrs Bentley were just regaling us with tales of their recent trip to Egypt and I informed them of your affinity for all things Egyptian."

Elizabeth opened her mouth to speak just as Georgia approached, a handsome stranger at her side.

Conversations stuttered to a halt as Georgia's hand fluttered towards the Bentleys. "Of course, you already know this pair of reprobates."

The stranger stepped forward and grasped Mr Bentley's hand firmly. "A pleasure to see you both again." He turned to Mrs Bentley, lifting her fingers to his lips.

Mrs Bentley's cheeks reddened as the stranger straightened and faced the rest of the group.

Georgia gestured to each person in turn as she made the introductions. "And this is Lord William Hawthorne, his wife, Lady Caroline, Miss Meli Diomaros, and last but by no means least, Lady Elizabeth Hawthorne." She placed a hand on the stranger's arm. "Everyone, allow me to introduce Mr Enzo Bellini."

So this was the infamous Enzo Bellini. The man responsible for the tension between Georgia and Iggy. His handshake lingered as he reached her, her skin prickling as his dark eyes locked onto hers. "A pleasure to make your acquaintance." Enzo's voice caressed the words, his gaze never leaving Elizabeth's.

"Bellini?" William straightened, recognition dawning in his eyes. "The *Isotta Fraschini* importer?"

Enzo's lips curved in a satisfied smile. "The very same. I'm pleased my reputation precedes me."

"Indeed it does," William replied, his interest piqued. "I've heard remarkable things about the *Isotta Fraschini* models. The straight-eight engine, in particular, is said to be quite impressive."

"You have a keen ear for automotive excellence, Lord Hawthorne." Enzo slipped a card from his breast pocket. "Perhaps you'd be interested in experiencing it firsthand? I'd be delighted to arrange a test drive of our new Tipo 8A for you. A marked improvement over your current motorcar, I'm sure."

Caroline leaned closer, tapping William's hand with a playful glint in her eyes. "I beg you, Mr Bellini, not a word more about motorcars or we'll be here until sunrise."

"In that case, I'm afraid I must steal Mr Bellini away." Georgia's hand alighted on Enzo's arm. "I've promised him a tour of the stables, and I'd hate for Italian engineering to distract from our prize thoroughbreds."

William inclined his head, a chuckle escaping him. "Another time for the Tipo 8A, then."

"I look forward to it, Lord Hawthorne."

Elizabeth watched as Georgia led Mr Bellini away. There was something about him that both intrigued and unsettled her. His charm was undeniable, yet beneath it lurked a sharpness she couldn't quite place.

Like a beautiful motorcar with an engine that purred too smoothly – what secrets might it be hiding under its gleaming bonnet?

As if sensing her scrutiny, he paused at the doorway. He turned, looking back over his shoulder, his dark eyes finding hers across the room. For a heartbeat, their gazes locked, and Elizabeth felt a jolt of … something.

But before she could name it, he was gone.

Chapter Seven

GRAND NATIONAL DAY FEVER whipped Rosewood Park into a flurry of activity. The Rolls-Royce Silver Ghost and Georgia's ivory Vauxhall 30-98 stood ready to transport the Hawthornes and Fairfaxes to the hallowed turf of Aintree racecourse.

Georgia adjusted her driving gloves, settling behind the wheel of her Vauxhall. "Ready to hit the road? Time and the Grand National wait for no one, even if their grandmother was a cousin of Queen Victoria!" She cast a playful glance at her husband as he eased into the passenger seat, his cane resting across his lap.

"Is Iggy really related to Queen Victoria?" Meli asked, settling into her seat as Simmons closed the car door.

William arched an eyebrow, a hint of amusement playing across his features. "I believe so. Though I daresay Iggy would rather trek through the Amazon than take tea with the King."

Georgia's Vauxhall shot down the driveway in a blur of ivory, leaving a trail of dust and Simmons in her wake.

Simmons eased the Rolls-Royce into motion. William glanced at the receding dust cloud. "No wonder Iggy won't let her near his Aston Martin."

Hedgerows whipped by as Simmons guided the Rolls-Royce through winding country lanes. Elizabeth craned her neck, searching for a glimpse of ivory paintwork, but Georgia's Vauxhall remained elusive.

The pastoral quiet faded as they neared Aintree. A parade of motorcars and carriages clogged the roads, their passengers a riot of colourful hats and smart suits. Excited chatter drifted through open windows, punctuated by the occasional whinny of a nervous horse.

Aintree's grandstand loomed ahead, its red brick and ironwork showcasing the grandeur of Victorian architecture. Flags bearing the racecourse's logo fluttered atop the structure, adding splashes of colour to the scene.

Simmons brought the Rolls-Royce to a smooth stop as Iggy hobbled towards them, his walking stick tapping a staccato rhythm on the gravel. "Ah, there you all are," he called, his rich baritone carrying a hint of playful reproach. "I was about to send out a search party."

William's eyes crinkled with amusement. "The way Georgia took off, you'd think she was piloting one of those new Sopwith Snipes. I'm amazed Simmons didn't lose us in her slipstream."

Iggy's smile wavered. He shifted his weight, knuckles whitening around his walking stick. "Yes ... my wife tends to have little regard for the rules of the road."

"Where's Georgia? I thought she'd be with you." Caroline changed the subject as if sensing the change in Iggy's mood.

Iggy's gaze darted towards the stables. "With Tommy." His jaw tightened. "Discussing last-minute tactics, no doubt." He shifted his weight, knuckles whitening around his walking stick. "She insisted I wait here for you, but I think young Tanner will appreciate some familiar faces."

Elizabeth noted the stiffness in Iggy's shoulders, a stark contrast to the jubilant atmosphere around them.

Meli tugged at Elizabeth's sleeve, eyes shining. "Isn't this simply thrilling? I can scarcely wait for the race to begin!"

The corners of Iggy's mouth lifted, but the smile didn't reach his eyes. He tapped his walking stick against the gravel. "Come. Let's see how our young jockey is faring."

Iggy set off towards the stables, William falling into step beside him.

Grooms darted between stalls as they neared the stables. Horses stomped and snorted, their hooves clattering against the wooden floors. Tack jingled as stable hands adjusted bridles and saddles. A mare's shrill whinny cut through the din of shouted instructions and murmured conversations.

Iggy navigated the narrow aisle, his cane sliding slightly on the damp, straw-strewn floor. William and Caroline kept pace beside him, while Elizabeth and Meli hung back. Meli's eyes widened at the commotion, wrinkling her nose as the pungent mix of horse and manure assailed her senses. Elizabeth touched her cousin's elbow, guiding her past a pile of fresh straw.

Iggy pointed his cane towards a lean figure in a set of teal and gold racing silks brushing down a sleek bay gelding. "Ah, there's our young Tanner."

The boy's head snapped up, eyes widening. He dipped his head in a bashful nod. "Lord Hawthorne, sir. Lady Hawthorne. Lord Fairfax."

William stepped forward, his eyes crinkling. "Your parents send their best wishes, Alfie. As does my aunt, Lady Beatrice."

A flush crept up Alfie's cheeks. "Th-thank you, sir. I'll do my best to make everyone proud." His gaze darted between them and the horse.

William's hand landed on Alfie's shoulder with a gentle pat. "I'm sure you will."

"And do be careful," Caroline said, her brows knitting together. "Particularly at Becher's Brook. I hear it's unseated even the most experienced riders."

"Don't worry, Lady Hawthorne." Alfie's hand moved to the gelding's shoulder. "Tommy's had me and Sir Gallant practicing day and night for that jump."

Meli's fingers stretched towards the horse's muzzle. "Sir Gallant? Is that his name?" Her hand jerked back suddenly.

"You're alright with this one, miss." Alfie's lips quirked into a small smile. "He's as gentle as a lamb. No danger of him biting you."

Iggy's eyebrow arched. "Ah, you've met Tempest then?"

Meli eyed the stalls warily. "Yes, she almost gave me quite a nip."

"Another fiery redhead ... just like her owner." Iggy's jaw tightened for a moment, a shadow passing over his features.

"And speaking of my wife, has Lady Fairfax been by to see you yet?" Iggy's voice lightened, any trace of previous unease smoothed away.

Alfie's eyes brightened. "Yes, sir. She was here not a half hour since. Came to wish me luck for the race."

Iggy's hand settled on Alfie's shoulder. "Well, we won't keep you from your preparations, my boy. Just do your best out there. That's all anyone can ask."

A nervous smile spread across Alfie's face. "Thank you, Lord Fairfax, sir. I will."

William stepped forward, his gaze warm on Alfie. "And remember, Tanner, we're all rooting for you."

As the group bid Alfie farewell, they made their way back towards the grandstand. The crowd at Aintree swelled around them, excited shouts mingling with the thunderous rhythm of hooves pounding turf and distant cries of bookies hawking odds.

Elizabeth found herself drifting away from William, Caroline, and Iggy, Meli's arm clutched tightly in her own.

She paused near the betting stands, trying to get her bearings. Her gaze drifted across the sea of faces, settling on the familiar figure of Reggie Black.

Reggie's voice carried over the din, his smile casual. "Hey, Doc, why don't you tell us which horse you put your money on? Save us all from backing a loser!"

Elizabeth's eyes followed Reggie's line of sight to the stiff form of Dr Edward Franklin. Colour drained from his face, his features twisting.

Reggie's smirk widened before he turned and strutted off in the direction of the stables.

A rich Italian accent sliced through the cacophony of the racetrack. "Lady Elizabeth, Miss Meli, what a delight!"

Elizabeth whirled around, her eyes landing on Enzo Bellini. He cut a dashing figure in his charcoal suit, weaving through the crowd with the grace of a panther. At his side strode a familiar face that made Elizabeth's breath hitch – Jonathan Ashcroft.

Bellini seized their hands, pressing his lips to their knuckles in turn with theatrical flair. "I'd begun to think Aintree had lost its charm, but here you are, proving me gloriously wrong."

Elizabeth extricated her hand, forcing a polite smile. "Mr Bellini, what a surprise."

"Allow me to introduce my associate, Mr Jonathan Ashcroft." Bellini gestured.

Jonathan's eyes met Elizabeth's, a flicker of something unreadable passing between them. "Lady Elizabeth. Miss Meli. A pleasure."

Meli's sharp intake of breath drew a quick, warning glance from Elizabeth. She inclined her head, playing along with Jonathan's feigned unfamiliarity. "Mr Ashcroft."

"I'm curious" – Jonathan's gaze darted between Elizabeth and Bellini – "how did two such charming ladies fall into the company of this scoundrel?" A hint of steel underlay his light tone.

Bellini's laugh rang out. "My dear Ashcroft, you wound me! Lady Elizabeth, pay him no mind. He's merely jealous of my natural charisma."

"We met at Rosewood Park." Elizabeth's eyes never left Jonathan's face. "A soiree hosted by Lady Fairfax. And you, Mr Ashcroft? Are you acquainted with the Fairfaxes?"

A muscle twitched in Jonathan's jaw. "I've had the pleasure of Lady Fairfax's company on occasion. Lord Fairfax's reputation precedes him, though we've yet to meet."

"An oversight easily remedied" – Bellini's smile turned predatory – "especially now that Georgia and I are to be business partners."

Meli's fingers dug into Elizabeth's arm. "Look, William's summoning us. The race must be about to start."

Elizabeth glanced over her shoulder, spotting her brother's urgent gestures. "So he is. Gentlemen, if you'll excuse us?"

"But of course." Bellini doffed his hat with a flourish. "Until next time, ladies. I suspect we'll be seeing much more of each other, now that Rosewood Park and I have … mutual interests."

As Meli pulled her away, she cast one last glance at Jonathan. His face was an inscrutable mask, but his eyes burned with an intensity that left her both unsettled and intrigued.

Elizabeth and Meli climbed the steps, the crowd below surging like a restless sea. A flash of gold and teal caught Elizabeth's eye. Alfie, his jockey silks unmistakable, stood toe-to-toe with Reggie Black near a cluster of trees. Reggie's red and white silks blazed in contrast.

Alfie's fists clenched, his body coiled like a spring. In a blur of motion, he lunged forward, shoving Reggie hard. The older jockey reeled back. Before Reggie could recover, Alfie spun away, shouldering through the crowd.

Elizabeth's heart raced as she watched Alfie's furious retreat. He collided with a towering blackboard, sending it crashing to the ground. White chalk dust billowed, spectators scattering with startled cries. Alfie ploughed on, vanishing into the throng as men scrambled to right the fallen display.

Fighting against the tide of bodies, Elizabeth and Meli finally reached their private box.

Iggy's voice boomed over the din. "At last! I feared the masses had swallowed you whole."

Elizabeth's smile wavered. "A wrong turn. Thank heavens for Meli's sharp eyes."

They settled into their seats, fumbling with their field glasses.

"I was worried we'd miss the start."

Caroline leaned in, her touch steadying Meli's hands. "Just in time. Look, they're lining up now."

Iggy's gaze darted across the grandstand, his jaw tightening as Georgia appeared.

"Where have you been?" Irritation laced his words.

Georgia glided in and her lips grazed Iggy's cheek. "Darling, you know these events. Always fashionably late." She slipped into the seat beside him.

Iggy's fingers found hers, the tension in his shoulders melting away.

As one, the group lifted their binoculars. On the track below, the horses lined up at the starting line.

Meli's finger jabbed the air. "There's Alfie!"

Near the gate, a black horse reared and pranced, shattering the carefully aligned field.

Elizabeth's eyes narrowed. "What on earth?"

Georgia's lips thinned. "Diablo, Reggie Black's mount. Always the showman."

Grooms swarmed the skittish Diablo, coaxing him back into line. The crowd held its breath as the starter's flag rose, then dropped.

Hooves thundered, the roar of the crowd swelling as thirty horses charged towards the First Fence. Through her field glasses, Elizabeth watched muscles coil and release with each powerful stride.

Diablo's ebony form surged alongside Sir Gallant's bay flank, jostling for the lead. They soared over the obstacle, riders crouched low, silks billowing.

At Becher's Brook, the pack stretched. Elizabeth's breath caught as Alfie's steady hands guided Sir Gallant over the deceptive drop.

The second lap intensified. Reggie's and Alfie's mounts surged neck and neck over The Canal Turn and Valentine's Brook. Elizabeth's heart pounded in time with the thunderous hooves.

Diablo drifted closer to Sir Gallant. Reggie's elbow caught Alfie's shoulder. The young jockey fought to keep his mount steady as Reggie pressed on, elbows jabbing.

Approaching the last fence, Diablo veered sharply into Sir Gallant's path. Reggie's elbows drove into Alfie, desperate to unseat his rival. Alfie's focus remained unwavering, his horse matching him stride for stride.

At The Elbow, the horses surged side by side. Reggie leaned in, his elbow grazing Alfie's side. In a flash, Sir Gallant pulled ahead. Reggie, thrown off balance, tumbled from Diablo just before the crucial turn.

Alfie seized his chance, urging Sir Gallant forward. The bay's thunderous hooves carried them through The Elbow and straight towards the finish line.

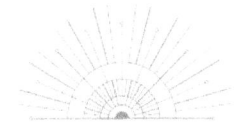

Chapter Eight

THE ROAR OF THE crowd swelled through Aintree's grandstand, a thunderous wave of cheers that set Elizabeth's heart racing. She watched, wide-eyed, as jubilant spectators hoisted Alfie aloft, his teal and gold silks a bright splash amidst the sea of faces.

Meli's fingers dug into Elizabeth's arm, her eyes wide and voice breathless. "Oh, Elizabeth! Alfie was simply magnificent!"

"He certainly was, Meli. I don't think any of us doubted him for a moment."

William's laughter boomed as he clasped Iggy's shoulder. "Tanner has done us all proud today."

Iggy steadied himself, his smile matching his friend's. "Indeed, he has."

"Alfie's performance will go down in history." Caroline's lips brushed her husband's cheek, her words full of pride.

Georgia whirled towards them, her auburn curls a fiery halo. She flung her arms around Iggy, nearly lifting him off his feet. "I knew that boy had it in him!"

Elizabeth and Meli pushed through the cheering crowd, struggling to keep pace with the rest of the party as they headed for the winner's enclosure. Georgia forged ahead, her long strides eating up the distance, intent on claiming her victory.

Well-wishers swarmed around them, slowing their progress. Georgia's voice rose above the crowd, her excitement sharpening her Texan accent as she greeted old friends and accepted their praise. Iggy pumped hands vigorously, accepting hearty backslaps from old acquaintances.

Meli grabbed Elizabeth's arm. "I never realised the Fairfaxes knew so many people here."

Elizabeth turned to her cousin. "Iggy's family have lived in Rosewood Park for generations.

And as we discovered earlier, their influence and connections reach far beyond Aintree."

As they neared the enclosure, Elizabeth spotted Alfie amidst a sea of reporters. The young jockey stood tall, his chin lifted as he fielded questions with newfound confidence. Georgia quickened her pace, making a beeline for Sir Gallant.

As they neared the enclosure, the cheers faded, replaced by an uneasy silence.

Meli's fingers dug into Elizabeth's arm. "What's happening?"

Elizabeth followed her cousin's gaze. Near the final stretch, a cluster of officials in dark suits and white-coated medical personnel huddled around something on the ground. The once-jubilant crowd now stood stock-still, their faces pale and drawn.

Iggy's pace slowed. "Good Lord," he murmured, the colour draining from his face.

Georgia's smile melted.

As they drew closer, Elizabeth noticed a figure lying motionless on a stretcher, a blanket draped over their form.

Her breath caught in her throat, a cold knot of dread settling in the pit of her stomach. "No." The word escaped her lips in a hushed, disbelieving whisper.

The news of Reggie's death rippled through the Aintree crowds. Journalists swarmed, their faces a mix of shock and professional urgency as they vied for interviews. Some rushed to the telephones, while others hurried away, scribbling in notepads as they raced to break the story.

"Broke his neck, they say," one reporter muttered to another.

Alfie remained rooted to the spot, his Grand National victory forgotten. His shoulders slumped, the weight of the tragedy visible in his posture. Tommy appeared at the young jockey's side and placed a hand on Alfie's arm.

Tommy glanced at Iggy and William, the lines around his eyes deepening. "I'll see the lad home."

Iggy's mouth tightened, the day's triumph now overshadowed. William's jaw clenched as he met his friend's gaze, both men sharing in the loss.

"The poor boy," Iggy murmured.

William nodded, and without further discussion, the Hawthornes and Fairfaxes departed for Rosewood Park, any thoughts of celebrating abandoned.

Hushed whispers and downcast faces followed them as they made their way to the motorcars. Once settled inside, Simmons eased the Rolls-Royce onto the road, joining the sombre trickle of vehicles leaving the racecourse.

Elizabeth gazed out the window, the passing landscape a blur of muted greens and greys. The earlier bustle of race-goers had vanished, replaced by a heavy silence that hung over the country lanes.

Inside, silence reigned. William's jaw remained tight, his hand clasped firmly in Caroline's. Meli sat unnaturally still, her usual chatter silenced.

Ahead, Georgia's Vauxhall moved at an uncharacteristically sedate pace. The cloud of dust that had trailed behind them on their journey to Aintree conspicuously absent.

As Rosewood Park came into view, its grand facade seemed to loom rather than welcome.

The motorcars pulled to a stop, and Elizabeth watched as Iggy emerged, his movements stiff and laboured.

For a moment, they stood in silent communion at the foot of the steps as if unsure how to proceed.

"I don't know about you lot." Georgia's voice cut through the stillness. "But I sure could use a stiff drink right now."

Pritchard materialised in the doorway and took their coats with a slight bow as they made their way to the drawing room.

William and Iggy gravitated towards the fireplace, while Georgia headed straight for the drinks cabinet.

"Whisky all round?" Georgia asked, already reaching for the crystal decanter. "We could all use a little pick-me-up."

Elizabeth accepted the tumbler from Georgia and sank into an armchair. Beside her, Meli sipped her drink, grimacing as the liquid settled on her tongue, she promptly discarded it.

William broke the silence, his voice low. "I still can't quite believe it."

Iggy nodded his agreement, his gaze fixed on the flickering flames.

"The sport isn't without its risks," Georgia remarked, draining her glass. "Even the best riders can't control everything."

Elizabeth caught Caroline's eye. Her sister-in-law's eyebrows arched, mirroring her own surprise at Georgia's blunt assessment.

Iggy's head snapped up. "For God's sake, Georgia, a man lost his life today."

Georgia's grip tightened around her glass, but she didn't look up as she set it back on the table. "I know … I was there, remember?"

Iggy's eyes narrowed, the muscle in his jaw twitching as their gazes locked.

"Yes, it's sad, but every one of those jockeys knows what they're getting themselves into." Her shoulders slumped as she exhaled, her voice taking on an edge as she continued. "But believe me, if Reggie Black could have chosen his way out, this would have been it."

Iggy's chest expanded in short, controlled bursts, his posture unnaturally stiff and eyes fixed on Georgia.

The silence stretched taut like a piano wire tuned too sharply.

Elizabeth's gaze darted between Iggy and Georgia. She opened her mouth when a short rap on the door drew everyone's attention.

Pritchard crossed the room with swift precision and leaned close to whisper in Iggy's ear. The shift in the air was instant – shoulders dropped, jaws unclenched. Moments later, the door swung wide, and in strode a stocky, middle-aged man, flanked by two constables.

"Chief Inspector Wainwright, to what do we owe this unexpected pleasure?" The saccharine sweetness in Georgia's tone did little to disguise her displeasure.

"Just some routine enquiries, Lady Fairfax." Wainwright's words were clipped, his moustache twitching.

Georgia's eyes flashed. "Surely it can wait. The poor boy's barely had time to catch his breath since ... since it happened."

"A man is dead, Lady Fairfax." Wainwright's voice hardened. "And it's my job to find out why."

"Reggie Black fell from his horse. Plain and simple." Georgia's voice rose, her hands gesturing emphatically. "Hundreds of spectators saw it happen."

Wainwright's gaze slid to Iggy, his tone shifting to one of practiced reasonableness. "With all due respect, Lady Fairfax, the law demands a thorough investigation, regardless of ... connections." He paused, allowing his words to sink in. "As a magistrate, Lord Fairfax, you understand the importance of impartiality. We wouldn't want anyone to think justice was being ... obstructed."

Iggy's jaw tightened, caught between his wife and his official duties. "Of course," he replied, his eyes meeting Georgia's defiant gaze.

"Where's the lad now? Stables?" Wainwright's eyes narrowed, already moving towards the door.

Iggy stepped forward. "Yes. I'll show you the way."

"Best not, Lord Fairfax." Wainwright's tone was firm. "Your position as magistrate ... wouldn't want to compromise the investigation, would we?"

Elizabeth caught William's eye. "Perhaps Lord Hawthorne should accompany you instead. After all, Alfie and his family have strong connections to our family estate."

"Quite right," William agreed, his voice carrying a note of authority. "And Lady Elizabeth will join us to keep a record of the proceedings."

Wainwright's lip curled. "This isn't a social call, Lord Hawthorne. My constables are perfectly capable of taking notes."

William drew himself up. "As a magistrate, I find it often helps to have an impartial account."

Wainwright's jaw clenched. "Very well, Lord Hawthorne. If you and your secretary are ready, I'm a very busy man."

Elizabeth bristled at Wainwright's condescension. "Secretary, indeed," she murmured, falling into step with her brother.

William's lips twitched with the ghost of a smile as they led the way towards the stables, Wainwright and his constables following close behind.

Tommy looked up from his worn armchair as they entered his modest workspace.

"Where's Tanner?" Wainwright barked before Tommy could even rise to his feet.

Elizabeth winced at the inspector's tone, but Tommy seemed unfazed. "Thought it best to keep the lad busy, sir. He's down in the stalls, tending to the horses."

Without so much as a nod of acknowledgement, Wainwright turned on his heel and marched towards the stalls. Elizabeth exchanged a quick, disapproving glance with William before they followed, leaving Tommy to sink back into his chair with a weary sigh.

Elizabeth noticed Alfie's hackles rise the moment he spotted Wainwright. The curry brush in his hand stilled, Sir Gallant's coat half-groomed as Alfie turned to face the Chief Inspector.

Wainwright's gaze raked over Alfie, from his mud-splattered boots to his tousled hair. "Quite the race today, wasn't it, Tanner? You must be feeling very pleased with yourself?"

Alfie's gaze flicked to William, then back to Wainwright. His fingers tightened around the brush. "I suppose…"

"You must be," Wainwright pressed, edging closer. The acrid scent of tobacco preceded him. "Beating the great Reggie Black? That's no small feat for a newcomer like yourself."

Alfie's shrug did little to mask the tension in his shoulders. His fingers flexed around the brush handle.

"Tell me, Tanner" – Wainwright's voice took on a razor's edge – "did you and Black get along? I imagine there was some rivalry between you two."

Alfie's boot scuffed at the hay, his gaze fixed on the stable floor. "I didn't know him that well."

Elizabeth tracked Wainwright's every move, each word and gesture feeding her silent analysis.

Wainwright's eyes glinted as he circled Alfie, his voice low and menacing. "Black had quite the reputation. Rubbed people the wrong way, didn't he? I imagine that got under your skin."

Alfie's knuckles whitened around the curry brush. "I didn't pay any mind to what he said."

"Come now." Wainwright leaned closer, a sneer twisting his lips. "A champion like Black must've been frustrating for a young lad like you, desperate to prove himself."

"It wasn't like that." Alfie's jaw tightened, a muscle twitching beneath his skin.

Wainwright pressed on, his voice rising. "Jealousy's a powerful thing, Tanner. Is that what you were arguing about? Is that why you gave him that shiner?"

"Chief Inspector," Elizabeth interjected, her tone sharp as cut glass. "Mr Black's injury was the result of a dispute with Mr Archer, not Alfie. We have several witnesses who can confirm this."

"I stand by my sister's word, Wainwright," William interjected, his tone brooking no argument. "Perhaps it would be more prudent to pursue that line of inquiry instead."

Wainwright's moustache twitched as he turned to Elizabeth, his eyes narrowing. "It seems you've forgotten your notebook, Lady Elizabeth."

Elizabeth met his gaze unflinchingly, a hint of a smile playing at her lips. "So I have. But not to worry, my memory serves me well enough, Chief Inspector."

The Chief Inspector wheeled back to Alfie, his eyes boring into the young jockey. "I've got witnesses who saw you elbowing Black during the race. Care to explain your unsportsmanlike conduct?"

Alfie's composure finally cracked, his voice rising in frustration. "I didn't ... Reggie started it! He kept driving Diablo into Sir Galant, trying to unseat me. I had to stop him."

Silence fell over the stable, broken only by the soft nickering of horses and the rustle of hay underfoot. Elizabeth held her breath, the air thick with unspoken accusations.

"Did you deliberately push Reggie Black off his horse, Tanner?" Wainwright's words sliced through the air like the crack of a gunshot.

Alfie hesitated, his eyes darting between Elizabeth and William.

Wainwright's words fell like a death knell. "Alfred Tanner, I'm arresting you on suspicion of murdering Mr Reginald Black."

The room seemed to tilt, the words echoing in the stunned silence.

Alfie staggered back, colour draining from his face. His eyes found Elizabeth's, wide and desperate, as the constables closed in.

Chapter Nine

A**LFIE'S EYES, WIDE WITH** shock, darted between Elizabeth and William as Wainwright's words ricocheted off the stable walls. The young jockey stumbled backwards, his curry brush clattering to the floor. "No," he choked out. The constables moved with grim efficiency as they closed in. He flinched, twisting away, but their hands clamped down on his arms, unyielding as iron shackles.

The confident young jockey who'd thundered across the finish line of the Grand National was gone. In his place stood a terrified boy, his eyes locking onto William. "Lord Hawthorne, sir, you have to believe me," Alfie pleaded, words tumbling out in a desperate rush.

Elizabeth fixed her gaze on the cruel bite of metal against Alfie's wrists. "Chief Inspector, surely these aren't necessary."

Wainwright's moustache twitched as he turned to her. "Murder is a serious crime, Lady Elizabeth. We can't take chances."

"For goodness' sake, Chief Inspector." Elizabeth's breath hitched as she spoke. "He's not a murderer! He's barely more than a child."

Wainwright's nostrils flared as a bitter laugh escaped his lips. "Tell that to Harry Thornton."

"Harry Thornton?" William echoed.

"Owns Thornton's Pawnbrokers in town." Wainwright jabbed a finger towards Alfie. "This *child* attacked him during a robbery. Struck him from behind, like a coward. Old Harry didn't know what hit him."

Alfie's focus stayed stubbornly on the ground, his body tense. Elizabeth flicked a quick look at William, her brow lifting slightly in question.

"We'll be right behind you to the station." William placed a hand on Alfie's shoulder, his grip firm. "We'll get to the bottom of this, Tanner. You have my word."

Wainwright marched towards the house, his back rigid. Alfie shuffled behind, a constable on each side.

William touched Elizabeth's arm. "I'll ask Iggy about borrowing a motorcar. No need to trouble Simmons."

Elizabeth nodded. "I'll fetch my bag and coat."

Minutes passed before a navy-blue Aston Martin A3 rounded the corner and rolled to a stop.

"Blasted Rolls has a puncture." He climbed out, letting out a low, appreciative whistle as he ran a hand over the sleek hood. "Iggy said we could take his baby but told me to treat it like the crown jewels."

"Isn't she a beauty?" Elizabeth's hand hovered over the chrome as she shot her brother a coaxing smile. "Please, William. I'll be extra careful, I promise. Iggy will never know."

William's gaze flicked from Elizabeth's pleading eyes to the polished dashboard. "Very well," he muttered. "But for heaven's sake, remember these country lanes are not Brooklands."

"Really, William, anyone would think you didn't trust me behind the wheel." She slid into the driver's seat and her fingers caressed the leather-wrapped steering wheel.

The engine rumbled as the car rolled forward, gravel scattering beneath the tyres as they trailed the Chief Inspector. William's fingers clenched around the edge of his seat as the countryside blurred in a dizzying rush.

The Aston Martin eased to a stop, the engine purring as it settled. Elizabeth shot William a playful glance. "You can open your eyes now."

William smoothed his windblown hair, a reluctant grin creeping onto his face. "I swear, you'll have me grey before my next birthday."

Elizabeth laughed as they headed up the steps to the station. "You've been saying that since I got my first motorcar."

The desk sergeant eyed them for a moment before disappearing down a corridor.

Elizabeth felt William's impatience beside her, his fingers drumming against the counter as they waited.

After what seemed like an eternity, the sergeant returned, his expression unreadable. "The Chief Inspector is busy, but he'll see you when he can. You can take wait or come back tomorrow."

"Thank you, Sergeant." She glanced around the sparse, utilitarian space – the hard wooden benches, the barred windows – the air thick with the scent of ink and stale tobacco making her nose twitch.

Guiding William towards one of the benches, she leaned in, her voice lowered. "I suspect the Chief Inspector doesn't take kindly to outsiders telling him how to do his job."

William's brow creased as he settled onto the wooden strip. "Indeed, it certainly seems that way."

The door to Wainwright's office swung open. The detective stepped out, his face set in a scowl. "Lord Hawthorne, Lady Elizabeth." His voice was low and rough. "Still here, I see."

He handed a stack of papers to an officer, his attention shifting back to them. "With all due respect, Lord Hawthorne. I know why you're here, but I want to be clear. I won't have a couple of toffs from London thinking they can meddle in my investigation or tell me how to do my job."

Elizabeth straightened, her smile cool and composed as she met Wainwright's gaze. "Of course not, Chief Inspector. A man of your experience needs no instruction." Her hazel eyes remained steady. "But Alfie's parents have worked for our family for years. We owe it to them to ensure he's treated fairly."

Wainwright's jaw tightened, irritation flashing in his eyes. "Very well." His voice came out strained. "But don't think for a moment that your rank will change the outcome."

Beside her, William shifted, tension rippling through his posture. Before he could speak, Elizabeth placed a light hand on his arm, her voice smooth as silk. "We wouldn't dream of it, Chief Inspector. We're here as observers, nothing more."

Wainwright's eyes narrowed, his jaw twitching, but after a pause, he jerked his head towards the office. "Then follow me."

The siblings shared a quick glance, heavy with unspoken words, before following the detective.

Wainwright yanked open the door to the interview room. Elizabeth slipped in behind him,

William at her heels. Her eyes darted to Alfie, his slight frame hunched over the scarred table, a constable looming nearby.

Lowering himself into the chair across from Alfie, Wainwright flicked his eyes towards Elizabeth and William, then snapped at the constable. "Chairs."

"Right, Tanner." Wainwright's voice cut straight to the point. "Let's talk about your history with Black."

Alfie's fingers twisted together, knuckles white as his gaze stayed locked on the table. "H-He was always ... always at me. Kept saying ... I wasn't any good. Told me... told me to clear off, go back where I came from." His eyes darted to William before dropping again. "Said ... said I was only here 'cause some nob felt sorry for me." He swallowed hard. "No offense, Lord Hawthorne."

William inclined his head, his face betraying nothing.

Wainwright's chair creaked as he leaned forward, eyes boring into Alfie. "What about during the race? Witnesses say you were pushing Reggie."

Alfie's fingers curled into fists. "That's not … It wasn't like that, sir. Reggie kept forcing Diablo into Sir Gallant. He was leaning on me, trying to unseat me."

"That's not what my witnesses said." Wainwright's voice cut like a knife.

"They're lying," Alfie shot back, his jaw clenching.

Wainwright's eyebrows arched. "All of them? Why would they do that?"

"I don't know, do I?" Alfie's voice cracked. "But that's not what happened."

"So you're telling me" – Wainwright's words dripped with sarcasm – "that all these people are lying and you didn't push Reggie Black?"

"No … yes–" Alfie stammered, his face flushing.

Wainwright pounced, his voice rising. "Yes? No? Which is it? Yes, you pushed Reggie Black from his horse? No, the witnesses aren't lying?"

"No … I don't–" Alfie's eyes darted around the room, his breath coming in short gasps. "You're confusing me."

Elizabeth's breath caught. Her eyes darted to William, finding his jaw clenched, his expression inscrutable. Poor Alfie was floundering against Wainwright's onslaught.

"Finding it hard to keep track of your lies, Tanner?" Wainwright's lip curled. He waved his hand, dismissing Alfie's words.

"I'm not lying." Alfie's fist ground into his palm. "I told you, Reggie was pushing me, forcing his horse into Sir Gallant … It was him, not me."

Wainwright leaned in, his voice low and menacing. "Admit it. Reggie was right – you were out of your depth. A kid like you riding in the National? Did he say something that made you snap, made you push him?"

"No, I–"

"Save it." Wainwright cut him off. "You've got motive, means, and opportunity to get rid of Reggie, to win the race. All the pieces fit."

As Wainwright pressed on, Alfie's shoulders tensed, his eyes flashing with defiance. "I'm telling you, I didn't do it…"

Elizabeth's fingers dug into William's arm, her eyes silently pleading with him to intervene.

"Chief Inspector, the boy clearly needs a break."

"To concoct more lies? This is a murder investigation, Lord Hawthorne, not afternoon tea."

A sharp knock silenced the room. "Enter!" Wainwright barked.

A constable entered and leaned close to whisper in the detective's ear. Wainwright's eyes lit up, a wolfish grin spreading across his face as he snatched a stack of papers from the constable's hands.

Wainwright's fingers flew through the documents, his gaze darting between them. With a satisfied grunt, he slapped them onto the table, spreading them out for all to see.

Elizabeth's breath caught. Photographs. Clear, damning images of Sir Gallant pressed against Diablo, Alfie's arm outstretched towards Reggie.

"Well, well, Tanner." Wainwright's voice oozed satisfaction. He jabbed a gnarled finger at the photographs. "Care to explain these?"

Alfie's gaze jumped from Elizabeth to William, his face drained of all colour. Elizabeth's gut twisted as the damning photos stared back at her.

"Alfred Tanner, you're under arrest for the murder of Reginald Black," Wainwright said coldly, his eyes hard. A quick nod to the constable. "Take him down."

"Is it really necessary to lock him up, Chief Inspector? Surely he can stay under Lord Fairfax's supervision while the investigation proceeds? There's no need for this."

Wainwright barely spared him a glance, his expression hard. "This isn't a minor charge, Lord Hawthorne. You of all people should know that. The lad's accused of murder, not trespassing. He stays where I can keep an eye on him."

"We'll sort this, Tanner … just hang in there."

The constable took hold of Alfie, but his desperate eyes never left Elizabeth. She tried to speak, but the words wouldn't come. All she could do was watch as he was led away.

Shaking off the sinking feeling, Elizabeth turned her attention back to the photos spread across the table. Her gaze lingered over the images. "These photos don't prove anything." She pointed to one, her voice tense. "Diablo's all over the place, forcing Sir Gallant off course in several of them. If anything caused Mr Black to fall, then I'd say it was Diablo."

Wainwright's pen hovered, tapping lightly on the edge of his notepad. "Tanner's trouble. It was just a matter of time before he ended up behind bars." He set the pen down, slow and deliberate. "And if certain folks hadn't meddled, he'd already be locked up for what he did to old Harry Thornton, and Black would still be alive."

"Harry Thornton?" Elizabeth kept her voice even. "I'm afraid we're not familiar with that name, Chief Inspector."

Wainwright's gaze bore into her. "I'm not surprised. Lady Fairfax seemed rather keen to keep it quiet." He leaned forward, voice low. "A few months back, Tanner broke into Thornton's Pawnshop. Old Harry caught him, and the lad walloped him from behind before scarping."

William's grip tightened on the table's edge. "And Mr Thornton's condition?"

Wainwright's lips pressed into a thin line. "He spent a few days in hospital, but it could've been much worse if his son hadn't found him."

Elizabeth's lips parted in surprise. "That doesn't sound like Alfie. Are you sure your witness wasn't mistaken?"

"Sam Thornton saw him clear as day. Knows him from the Fairfax stables," Wainwright shot back.

"If you were so convinced of Alfie's guilt, why didn't you charge him?" William asked.

Wainwright's eyes flicked to the photos on the table. "Pressure from above. I was told to drop it."

Elizabeth's brow creased. "Are you implying Lord and Lady Fairfax had something to do with this?"

Wainwright shrugged, barely looking at her. "Make of it what you will." He stood, expression unreadable. "Now, if you'll excuse me, some of us have real work to do."

The station's clamour faded as they stepped outside, the weight of Wainwright's words hanging between them.

Without a word, Elizabeth made for the passenger side of the Aston Martin, her shoulders slumped. William slid behind the wheel, the engine's gentle purr filling the silence.

"What happens to Alfie now?"

William's grip tightened on the steering wheel. "He'll stay here until the Liverpool Assizes convene."

"When will that be?" Elizabeth turned to her brother, searching his face.

"A week, give or take. Depends on their docket."

They continued on in silence, the country lanes winding past, unnoticed by Elizabeth as Wainwright's accusations echoed in her mind. William's voice cut through her thoughts.

"I'll make some telephone calls in the morning. We need to plan Alfie's defence and find proper legal counsel." His eyes darted to Elizabeth.

She turned to him. "What do you make of Wainwright's claims about Alfie and this Mr Thornton?"

"Iggy mentioned Alfie had trouble settling in when he first arrived. But after Tommy took him under his wing, he seemed to find his way."

Elizabeth recalled Alfie's clenched jaw and fierce glare as he'd faced off with Reggie in the stables. "Do you really think Alfie would break into a shop and attack the owner?"

"Normally, I'd say no." He exhaled slowly. "But seeing how he reacted to Wainwright's questioning, I suppose if Alfie felt corned, he might have lashed out."

Elizabeth's stomach twisted. Alfie wasn't violent by nature, but trapped, he might act rashly. Had that been the case during the race?

As Rosewood Park loomed ahead, Elizabeth stared at the passing greenery, her mind churning with questions. Each one inched her closer to an unsettling possibility – was Alfie guilty?

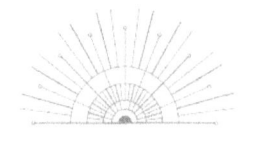

Chapter Ten

SILENCE BLANKETED THE MORNING room at Rosewood Park, broken only by the occasional clink of a silver teaspoon against a china teacup. Elizabeth's gaze swept over the sombre faces around the breakfast table, a grim reminder of how swiftly Reggie's death and Alfie's subsequent arrest upended their world.

Untouched toast cooled on gilt-edged plates, and half-eaten kippers congealed, their once-enticing aroma now stale and unappetising. Even Meli, whose vibrant energy typically infused any room with warmth, sat rigidly in her chair. Her shoulders hunched forward as she toyed listlessly with a napkin, her eyes fixed on some distant point beyond the table. Across from her, William's jaw clenched and unclenched as he stared unseeing at his discarded breakfast, while Caroline's hands clasped tightly around her teacup, her gaze flicking anxiously between her husband and the others.

The heavy silence stretched on, broken only by a discreet cough from the doorway that drew everyone's attention. Pritchard stood ramrod straight, his usually impassive face betraying a hint of apology for the interruption.

"My lord," he addressed William, his voice low and measured. "There's a telephone call for you, sir. The caller insisted it was most urgent."

William's expression tightened. He glanced at Caroline before pushing back his chair. "Very well, Pritchard. I'll come at once."

As he passed, William's hand briefly squeezed his wife's shoulder, a fleeting gesture of reassurance. Elizabeth watched her brother's retreat, noting the slight stoop to his usually impeccable posture, betraying the strain of recent events.

The door clicked shut behind him, leaving the room in an even more pronounced state of unease. Elizabeth caught Meli's eye across the table, seeing her own questions mirrored in her cousin's worried gaze. Who could be calling at this hour? Her mind immediately turned to Alfie. Had something happened to him?

As if reading their minds, Iggy leaned forward slightly. "I'm sure it's something to do with William's work. Probably some pressing judicial matter demanding his attention. With the economic strain after the war, crime has been on the rise, leaving magistrates stretched particularly thin."

Elizabeth nodded. "I'm sure you're right, but I can't help but worry about Alfie." Her gaze swept across the faces at the table. "Chief Inspector Wainwright seems to have such a dislike for anyone with a title that I'm unsure whether our involvement might be more hindrance than help."

Iggy's eyebrows shot up. "You've noticed that too, haven't you? I thought it was just me he'd taken a dislike to."

"Oh, it's not just you, honey," Georgia chimed in, her sea-green eyes flashing. "That man seems to have a real chip on his shoulder about everything. Heaven forbid anyone should have had the nerve to be born into privilege ... or a woman, for that matter."

Elizabeth's shoulders slumped as she exhaled, her breath carrying the weight of her concerns. "It's not just his disdain for the aristocracy that troubles me." Her gaze swept across the faces around the table. "His bias against Alfie worries me more. I'm afraid he's seeing foul play where none exists."

She leaned forward. "Do you know what happened between Alfie and Mr Thornton? Wainwright seems convinced Alfie attacked him during a burglary, but if that were true, surely Alfie would have been incarcerated?"

Iggy exhaled slowly, his gaze settling on some distant point beyond the window. "Wainwright visited Rosewood Park to question Alfie about the incident. But since nothing further came of it, I assumed he lacked any credible evidence." He paused briefly. "Or perhaps Sam Thornton had retracted his statement."

Georgia let out a soft snort. "I wouldn't put too much stock in anything Sam Thornton says." She glanced at Elizabeth. "That man's reputation is shadier than the elm grove behind our stables. I wouldn't be surprised if he realised his mistake once he sobered up."

Elizabeth's eyebrows arched at Georgia's candid assessment. "You think he might have been intoxicated when he made the accusation?"

"Wouldn't be the first time," Georgia replied matter-of-factly. "Sam Thornton has a bit of a reputation for overindulging at the local public house, if you catch my meaning."

Elizabeth stilled, Georgia's words sinking in. The pieces of the puzzle began to shift in her mind, casting Wainwright's actions in a new light. His claim of pressure from above to drop the Thornton investigation now rang hollow. Could it be that the Chief Inspector had simply lacked evidence? Given what Georgia had just revealed about Sam Thornton's drinking habits and questionable reliability, it seemed more likely that Wainwright simply hadn't had enough evidence to proceed.

The thought nagged at her. If Wainwright had misrepresented his reasons for abandoning that investigation, what else might he be twisting to fit his narrative? Was he trying to paint Black's accident as a murder in order to frame Alfie because he'd failed to secure a conviction for Harry Thornton's attack?

She frowned as she considered the implications. It seemed there were far more questions surrounding both cases than she'd initially realised.

The door creaked open, and William reappeared, his shoulders tense beneath his jacket. Elizabeth noted the tightness in his jaw and the way his fingers drummed against his thigh – telltale signs of his unease.

Caroline smoothed her napkin, her eyes searching her husband's face. "Is everything alright, William?"

"I'm afraid I've been called back to London on urgent judiciary business." He sighed, pinching the bridge of his nose. "It seems there's a rather complex case requiring immediate attention."

"Ah, the demands of duty. They wait for no man, unfortunately." Iggy offered William a sympathetic smile. "I'm sure they wouldn't have called if it wasn't absolutely necessary."

"I'm sure you're right."

"When will you be leaving?" Georgia asked.

"On the next train, I'm afraid. I've already asked Pritchard to make the necessary arrangements."

Getting to her feet, Elizabeth turned to Georgia. "Perhaps one of the maids could assist with the packing?"

William held up a hand. "Actually, Elizabeth, I'd prefer you to stay on until this matter with Alfie is resolved. And Meli, too, of course." His eyes met hers, conveying an unspoken plea. "I'm sure Iggy and Georgia won't mind."

Elizabeth hesitated, glancing between Iggy and Georgia. "We wouldn't want to impose."

"Nonsense, you're both welcome to stay as long as you need to. We have bags of room. Isn't that right, darling?" Iggy asked.

The smile faded briefly from Georgia's lips before she swiftly composed herself. "Sure ... sure thing, honey."

Elizabeth caught Georgia's smile faltering, a momentary ripple in the warm hospitality of Rosewood Park. She tucked the observation away as Caroline rose from her chair.

Caroline's gaze darted between William and the others. "I should prepare for our departure. Elizabeth, Meli, would you mind helping?"

Elizabeth nodded, answering for both of them.

As they neared the door, William cleared his throat. "Iggy, might I use your telephone? I've some calls to make before we leave."

Iggy gestured towards the hallway. "Help yourself."

The group dispersed, but William's fingers grazed Elizabeth's elbow as they exited the room.

"A word?" he murmured, his expression grave.

Elizabeth glanced at Meli and Caroline. "You two go ahead. I'll join you shortly."

Meli quirked a questioning brow before continuing upstairs with Caroline.

William guided her to a secluded corner, his posture rigid. "Alfie's predicament…"

"Don't worry, I'll see to it that Wainwright conducts a fair investigation. But there is something else that's bothering me … The Chief Inspector's witness in the Thornton assault isn't particularly credible according to Georgia, which makes me question whether Alfie was really involved at all."

A crease formed between William's brows as he considered her words. "Perhaps you could look into it while I'm away." He paused before letting out a sigh. "I expect this case will occupy most of my time, but if you need anything, send word. I'll assist however I can."

Elizabeth inclined her head in agreement. "You have my word."

William placed a hand on her shoulder, his gaze steady and serious. "I know I'm asking a lot, Elizabeth. The racing world can be a dangerous place, full of unsavoury characters and illicit activities. Just promise me you'll be careful."

A wry smile tugged at the corners of Elizabeth's lips. "Aren't I always?"

William chuckled softly, shaking his head. "That may be, but trouble does seem to have a knack for finding you."

The rest of the morning passed in a flurry of activity as William and Caroline prepared for their journey back to London.

Elizabeth hugged Caroline and then William, his parting words of caution still echoing in her ears. With a final wave from the assembled group, her brother and sister-in-law climbed into the Rolls-Royce. They all watched as Simmons steered the vehicle down the long driveway, the silver bodywork soon disappearing behind a row of ancient oaks.

As they drifted back inside, Elizabeth's mind turned to the investigation ahead, Georgia's words about Sam Thornton lingering in her thoughts.

"Meli," she said, looping her arm through her cousin's as they made their way up the stairs, "will you be alright here on your own this afternoon? I need to pay a visit to the police station."

"Of course," Meli agreed. "And anyway, Georgia has offered to teach me to ride."

She nodded, her mind already racing ahead to her visit to the police station. Once back in the bedroom, Elizabeth adjusted her peach-coloured cloche hat in the mirror before securing it with a pearl-tipped hatpin. Her eyes met her reflection, steely determination glinting beneath the embroidered brim.

She smoothed down the folds of her drop-waisted day dress, a light wool crepe in a soft sage green that brought out the flecks of green in her hazel eyes.

Meli sprawled across the bed, her chin propped on her hands. "Are you sure you don't want me to come with you to the police station?"

"I think it's best if I go alone this time," Elizabeth said, her eyes meeting Meli's in the mirror as she carefully applied a dash of rose-coloured lipstick.

Meli sat up on the bed. "Are you sure? I could postpone my riding lesson. I'm sure Georgia would understand."

Elizabeth turned to face her cousin with a grateful smile. "That's kind of you to offer, but I think it's better if I go alone. From what I've seen of Chief Inspector Wainwright, his dislike of women seems to be on par with his feelings about the aristocracy."

She capped her lipstick, catching sight of Meli's reflection. The excitement had faded from her cousin's face. "Meli? Whatever's the matter?"

Meli bit her lip. "Do you think Aunt Beatrice will be terribly cross about Alfie's arrest?"

Elizabeth paused to ponder her cousin's question before slipping her lipstick inside her cream leather clutch. "She'll be vexed about the public scrutiny, certainly. But Aunt Beatrice has weathered her fair share of storms over the years." She clicked the bag shut with a decisive snap. "Ultimately, I think she'll be more concerned about Alfie's fate and the worry it must be causing his poor parents."

"At least Caroline will be with them in a day or two to offer her support," Meli said, her face brightening.

Elizabeth nodded, her eyes warming at the mention of her sister-in-law. "Very true, and Caroline has such a gift for knowing exactly what to do in difficult times. I'm sure her presence will be a great comfort to Aunt Beatrice as well as the Tanners."

She adjusted the silk scarf knotted loosely at her throat, its design a blend of sage and peach hues in a fashionable art deco pattern. With a final glance in the mirror, Elizabeth turned towards the door.

"Meli," Elizabeth called out, her hand on the doorknob. "Enjoy your riding lesson and do try to stay out of trouble while I'm away."

Meli's laugh rang out, bright and clear. "I'll do my best, but no promises!"

Elizabeth shook her head, a smile tugging at her lips despite her concerns. She took a deep breath, steadying herself for the task ahead.

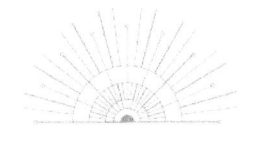

Chapter Eleven

Elizabeth eased Iggy's Aston Martin to a stop outside Aintree police station. As the engine quieted, Aintree's bustle intruded – horses' hooves clattered on cobblestones, newsboys shouted headlines, and a steam train whistled in the distance. Elizabeth adjusted her cloche hat in the rear-view mirror, swiped on a fresh coat of lipstick, and reached for the door handle.

She wrinkled her nose at the stench of stale tobacco smoke as she entered the station. Sharp scents of ink and sweat permeated the haze. Typewriters clattered an impatient tempo. Shrill telephone rings pierced the air, competing with a sergeant's gruff orders.

She approached the front desk. A burly constable stood guard, his eyes fixed on a teetering pile of papers, seemingly oblivious to the clamour of ringing telephones and muted conversations filling the station.

She glanced at the wall-mounted clock, its steady ticking underlining her urgency.

The man's head jerked up. "Can I help you, miss?"

Elizabeth met his gaze. "Good afternoon, Officer. I'd like to see Mr Alfie Tanner, if you please."

The constable's brow furrowed, a muscle twitching in his jaw. "I'm afraid that won't be possible, miss. Chief Inspector Wainwright's instructions were clear – no visitors for the lad."

Elizabeth weighed her options quickly. She needed to speak with Alfie, but alienating this man wouldn't help. She leaned in slightly, her voice low. "I understand, but it's rather urgent. Surely we could make an exception?"

The constable hesitated, his fingers drumming on the desk. His eyes flicked from Elizabeth to the corridor and back again. "I … I'm not sure I can–"

"I promise I won't stay long," Elizabeth pressed, her eyes never leaving his face.

The man's internal struggle played across his face. Finally, he sighed, leaning in close. "Five minutes. Round the back. Don't let anyone see you."

Elizabeth slipped out, her steps quick but measured as she made her way to the station's rear. The alley's quiet unnerved her after the clamour inside, each passing moment stretching longer than the last.

She waited, her ears straining – a distant laugh, the rumble of a passing motorcar. Just as doubt began to creep in, a metallic scrape broke the silence.

The door opened a crack. The constable peered out, his earlier bravado gone. "Five minutes," he muttered, ushering her in with a quick glance over his shoulder.

The constable led Elizabeth down a short, dimly lit hallway. The air grew cooler and dank as they descended a narrow staircase, the smell of mildew and sweat intensifying with each step.

At the bottom, they entered a small room lined with three iron-barred cells. A single bulb cast pale light across the grey floor, barely reaching the shadowy corners. From one cell came the soft sound of someone shifting on a wooden bench.

The constable stopped at the middle cell, keys clinking as he unlocked the door. "Remember, five minutes," he muttered, swinging it open.

Alfie's head snapped up, his eyes widening. "Lady Elizabeth." A momentary smile flashed across his face, his hunched shoulders visibly relaxing.

She settled onto the bench opposite him, noting his rumpled clothes and the dark smudges under his eyes. His fingers fidgeted with the frayed edge of his jumper, betraying his anxiety.

"How are you holding up, Alfie?" Elizabeth asked softly.

Alfie's gaze darted to the door before returning to her. He shrugged, his forced smile not quite reaching his eyes. "Oh, you know me, Lady Elizabeth. Tough as old boots, me." His gaze slid over her shoulder, scanning the space behind her.

"Isn't Lord Hawthorne with you?"

Elizabeth shook her head. "I'm afraid he had to return to London this morning on urgent business."

Alfie seemed to shrink before her eyes.

"But don't fret," Elizabeth added quickly. "I assure you, we're still doing everything possible to clear your name. And Lord Hawthorne is just a telephone call away, should we need him."

He swallowed, the subtle tension in his neck giving him away.

Elizabeth's heart ached as she studied him. He was barely more than a boy, trying so hard to act the man. But his forced bravado couldn't quite mask the fear in his eyes or the tremor in his hands. Did he truly understand what was at stake?

She pushed the grim thought aside, refusing to let her mind wander down that dark path.

She edged closer, her gaze locking onto his. "Alfie, I need you to recount the race again for me."

Alfie's shoulders slumped, but before he could protest, Elizabeth continued, her voice gentle but firm. "I know it must be tiresome to keep going over it, but even the smallest detail could prove crucial."

Alfie took a deep breath, his eyes fixed on a stain on the grimy floor. "It started off all right. Then Reggie began crowding me, pushing Diablo right up against Sir Gallant."

He paused. Sweat beaded on his forehead. "The horses were all bunched up tight. Not much room to move. I kept looking for a gap … to break free of the pack."

Elizabeth shuffled on the bench, her brow knitted as she listened.

"But Reggie wouldn't let up." Alfie's voice tightened. "He kept coming at me, shoving … trying to knock me off. I tried to push him away … but he just kept coming at me."

Alfie's gaze met Elizabeth's, his eyes distant with recollection. "I finally got away from him. Diablo seemed to drop back a bit. I … I looked over my shoulder." He exhaled shakily. "It all happened so fast … but he didn't fall 'cause of me. Honest, he didn't."

Elizabeth mulled over Alfie's account. His description painted a clear picture of a tragic accident, not murder. She wondered why Chief Inspector Wainwright seemed so determined to pursue this case against Alfie. There had to be more to it.

"Alfie, can you think of any reason why the Chief Inspector is so set against you?" she asked, her voice hushed so the constable wouldn't overhear them.

Alfie squirmed. "It's because of what happened at Thornton's shop."

Elizabeth cocked her head. "Thornton's shop? Can you tell me what happened?"

Alfie paused, his fingers plucking at his sleeve cuff.

Elizabeth inched closer. "Alfie, if I'm going to help you, you have to tell me the truth."

He inhaled deeply. "Wainwright's convinced I broke in and assaulted Mr Thornton. But I swear it wasn't me, Lady Elizabeth."

"Tell me what happened," Elizabeth coaxed.

"I sometimes help Mr Thornton with odd jobs," Alfie explained. "That night, I was there late, moving some stuff Sam – that's his son –

had ordered." His shoulders shifted slightly, a flicker of hesitation crossing his face. "Then ... come morning, Wainwright stormed into Rosewood Park. Claimed a witness had seen me bolting from the shop, and Mr Thornton was found inside, battered."

Elizabeth absorbed the new information. "And what about Sam Thornton? What do you know about him?"

Alfie's expression soured. "Sam's nothing but trouble. He's always quarelling with his father over money."

"Have these quarrels ever escalated to blows?" Elizabeth probed.

Alfie's lips parted to answer, but the constable's voice cut in. "Time's up, miss."

As she stood, Elizabeth gave Alfie's shoulder a final, reassuring squeeze. His fingers clung to hers for a moment, his eyes silently begging her not to leave.

Elizabeth's head tilted, her gaze reassuring. "Keep your chin up, Alfie. We'll soon get to the bottom of this, I promise."

Elizabeth emerged into the afternoon, the fresh air sweeping away the lingering stench that had permeated every nook of the police cell. The metallic clang as the bolts locked behind her underscored the urgency of her task.

Alfie's account still weighed heavily on her mind as she made her way down the street, her sights set on Thornton's Pawnbrokers.

The scruffy facade of Thornton's Pawnbrokers and Curios greeted Elizabeth on the bustling high street. Dusty windows displayed an eclectic array – an old gramophone, a tarnished silver tea set, and antique pocket watches that caught her eye. A faded gold sign above the entrance hinted at the diverse wares within.

Elizabeth nudged the door open, and a bell tinkled overhead. Musty odours of aged wood and old fabric enveloped her the moment she stepped inside. Clutter bombarded her vision. Shelves and display cases crowded the walls, overflowing with an eclectic mix of items. Ornate jewellery glinted next to tarnished silverware. Worn leather-bound books jostled for space with peculiar trinkets. The sheer volume of objects overwhelmed the senses.

Her gaze swept across the haphazard arrangement of merchandise. She picked up a tarnished silver-plated tea set, its once-gleaming surface now dulled with age. Turning over the price ticket, she stifled a gasp at the outrageous figure. She replaced it carefully, her fingers ghosting over a nearby picture frame. Its gilt surface felt suspiciously light, likely just cheap brass beneath a thin gold wash.

Her attention shifted to a shelf lined with leather-bound books. She pulled one out, noting its dusty exterior but suspiciously crisp pages. The price tag attached to it seemed more suited to a rare first edition than this obvious reproduction.

As she examined a chipped porcelain figurine with an equally inflated price, she pondered the shop's clientele. How many unsuspecting customers had been lured in by these antiques? She replaced the figurine, her mind whirring with questions about the owner's business practices.

A young man materialised from behind a cluttered display. His gaze raked over Elizabeth, his eyes widening slightly as they took in her polished appearance. He smoothed down his slightly rumpled waistcoat and cleared his throat. "Good afternoon, madam. Might I be of assistance?" he asked, his accent strained with an unfamiliar elegance.

Elizabeth's lips curved into a polite smile. Her gaze flicked around the shop, absorbing every detail. "I'm in search of a…" She paused, fingers brushing the edge of her silk scarf. A glint of gold from a distant case caught her eye. "Gift … a pocket watch, perhaps … for my fiancé."

The young man's eyebrows lifted slightly. He gestured towards the counter, his movements becoming more animated. "Certainly, madam. We possess a fine collection. If you'd be so kind as to follow me."

"Is Mr Harry Thornton available? He's always been so patient with my indecisiveness." She laughed lightly, her fingers fidgeting with her scarf. "I'm afraid I tend to spend an age deliberating over the simplest dilemmas."

Sam's smile faltered. "I'm afraid my father isn't in today. He's … recovering from a recent incident."

Elizabeth paused, studying Sam's face. "Of course. I can see the family resemblance now.

Your father has always spoken so warmly of you in the past."

Sam's eyebrows shot up, disbelief etched across his features. "That would be a first," he muttered, a bitter edge to his voice.

Elizabeth watched Sam's reaction carefully, noting the tension in his jaw and the slight narrowing of his eyes. She backpedalled smoothly. "Well, perhaps I exaggerate a smidgen, but I'm certain he must be very proud of you."

Sam snorted, his gaze hard. "If you say so, madam."

Elizabeth's fingers clenched around her clutch, her nails pressing into the supple leather. "This incident you mentioned … I do hope it wasn't too serious and Mr Thornton is making a swift recovery?"

Sam's shoulders drooped. "He's not as young as he used to be … you know how it is."

"I do, unfortunately." She inclined her head, weighing her next words. "Did anyone see what happened?"

"Not the attack." Sam's gaze skittered across the shop, landing anywhere but on Elizabeth.

"But it was a good job I came to check on him and saw the blighter run away."

"Fortunate, indeed." She tilted her head slightly, her tone casual but curious. "Do you happen to know what was taken?"

"Mainly cash. But no doubt other things will come to light in the coming months…"

Elizabeth caught the sheen of sweat on Sam's brow. "Were there any witnesses?"

He hesitated, his hand shaking as he reached for a display case of pocket watches. "Er … just me."

"Did you recognise him?" she pressed, her tone deliberately light.

"Yes … a young lad who works at one of those fancy estates." Sam's throat worked as he swallowed.

Elizabeth's eyes widened slightly. "Not the same young man the police have arrested in connection with Mr Black's death?"

Sam nodded, his gaze fixed on a crack in the floorboards.

"If only the police had arrested him then, perhaps…" She let the words hang in the air. "Do you know why they didn't ... given that you witnessed him fleeing the scene of the crime?"

A muscle jumped in Sam's cheek. "Her highness up at Rosewood gave him an alibi. Claimed he was working in the stables."

Georgia gave Alfie an alibi? Elizabeth's brow creased as she processed this new information. The omission from their breakfast conversation now took on a peculiar significance, aligning uncomfortably with Wainwright's claim of instructions from above to drop the case.

Sam's readiness to blame Alfie raised further questions. The young man's recent arrival and tenuous connection to Harry Thornton's shop certainly made him an easy target.

As she considered the layers of this growing mystery, something about this situation didn't quite add up.

The tinkle of the doorbell disturbed her musings. She followed Sam's gaze to a burly man in an ill-fitting suit. He loitered rather than browsed, his presence oddly out of place.

Sam's attention drifted, his gaze repeatedly flicking to the newcomer. Elizabeth noted his growing unease, his fingers tapping nervously on the counter.

"What about those watches we discussed?" She picked up a nearby watch from the counter and held it up to catch the light. The glint off its face momentarily blinded Sam, forcing his attention back to her.

He started. "Actually, I've just remembered" – his voice strained as he inched away from her towards the man – "we're expecting a new delivery of pocket watches at the end of the week. There's sure to be some beauties in there." He glanced anxiously at the burly man. "Why don't you come back next week and have a look?"

Elizabeth's eyes narrowed at his abrupt dismissal. She opened her mouth, determined to continue her subtle interrogation despite Sam's obvious desire for her to leave.

The bell tinkled again, cutting off Elizabeth's retort as Jonathan Ashcroft breezed in, his gaze sweeping the shop before landing on her.

"Lady Elizabeth." Jonathan's eyes flickered briefly to Sam before returning to her. "What a delightful surprise. It's been far too long."

Elizabeth paused, recalling their encounter just yesterday. "Mr Ashcroft, it is indeed … a surprise."

Jonathan moved closer, positioning himself between Elizabeth and the burly man. "Pure serendipity, I assure you." His eyes darted briefly to Sam before returning to Elizabeth. "I hope I'm not interrupting anything?" He continued without waiting for a reply. "I trust the Mayfields are keeping well?"

Elizabeth's gaze shifted between Jonathan and Sam, noting the shopkeeper's poorly concealed relief at the interruption. "The Mayfields are in fine fettle, last I spoke with Clemmi."

"Excellent! And the arrangements for Miss Bella's nuptials? Progressing smoothly, I trust?"

Elizabeth stilled. Bella's nuptials? Jonathan knew very well that Clemmi was the one who was engaged to be married, not her younger sister. What on earth was he up to?

"Perhaps we could continue our catch-up over tea?" Jonathan's eyes met Elizabeth's, his gaze imploring.

Elizabeth paused, considering the unspoken weight behind his words. Jonathan's offer wasn't merely about catching up. Of that she was certain. "That sounds lovely." She turned to Sam. "I'm afraid these timepieces haven't quite caught my eye, Mr Thornton. Perhaps another day, when you've new stock in."

Sam's tension ebbed away. "Of course, madam. Do come again."

As they stepped onto the bustling street, Elizabeth glanced back at the shop. Sam leaned in close to the burly man, their whispered exchange swallowed by the street's clamour.

Elizabeth arched an eyebrow. "Since when has matrimonial minutiae piqued your interest, Mr Ashcroft?"

"Oh, one does like to keep abreast of these things," Jonathan replied, a mischievous glint in his green eyes.

Elizabeth studied Jonathan's profile as they walked. He'd saved her life twice, risking his own without hesitation. Yet secrecy shrouded him like a second skin. His charm disarmed her, even as it set off internal alarms. During the Mayfield Manor affair, he'd slipped effortlessly into the role of investigator, revealing connections that still baffled her. Glimpses of his influence in government circles only deepened his mystique. A faint sigh escaped her lips. How on earth could she trust a man whose very presence both steadied and unsettled her?

Chapter Twelve

THE CAFé DOOR SWUNG open, its brass bell jingling as Elizabeth and Jonathan stepped inside. Hushed conversations and the rustle of newspaper pages filled the air, mingling with the aroma of freshly baked pastries. Several patrons glanced up, their gazes fleeting as they hunched over white linen tablecloths, sipping from steaming cups. A polished mahogany counter ran along one wall, its glass case displaying an array of cakes and pastries. Behind it, polished silver teapots and an ornate coffee pot caught the light. Bentwood chairs surrounded each table, while framed landscapes adorned the floral wallpaper.

A waitress in a crisp black and white uniform threaded her way through the tables. Her eyes lit up as she spotted Jonathan. "I kept your table for you, Mr Ashcroft." She glanced at Elizabeth, her fingers smoothing her apron. "And I've just brewed a fresh pot of tea like you asked."

Jonathan's eyes crinkled, a warm smile lighting up his face. "Thank you, that's perfect. You've been most helpful." His rich voice seemed to envelop the waitress, who ducked her head, a deep flush blooming on her cheeks.

Elizabeth's brows knitted together as she tried to make sense of Jonathan's actions. If he had planned to return to the café so soon, why had he bothered to leave in the first place? It didn't quite add up.

He led Elizabeth to a table by the window, the lace curtains framing the busy street outside.

As they took their seats, her gaze settled on Jonathan, watching as his eyes repeatedly darted to the window. The table's strategic position provided a clear view of the front entrance of the street outside, and it was clear Jonathan was keeping a close watch. But what, or who, was he watching?

The waitress returned, balancing her tray with ease. She set down a steaming teapot, arranged Elizabeth's tea service, and placed Jonathan's black coffee before him.

She offered the waitress a warm smile as she set their drinks down, while Jonathan barely acknowledged her presence, his attention fixed on the window. The waitress lingered for a moment before quietly retreating, leaving the two of them in a bubble of silence.

Elizabeth's eyes flicked between the steaming drinks, Jonathan's profile, and Thornton's shop across the street. The pieces fell into place: Jonathan's presence earlier, their hasty departure from Thornton's, this particular table. She straightened in her chair, eyes narrowing. Jonathan wasn't simply looking at the street – he was watching the shop.

She leaned forward, eyes narrowing. "For someone supposedly interested in discussing wedding plans, you seem rather fixated on that shop."

Jonathan's focus snapped back to her, a practiced smile curving his lips. "Just admiring the architecture."

She arched an eyebrow, scepticism lacing her words. "Come now, Mr Ashcroft. We both know there's more to it than that."

Jonathan shifted, his gaze flicking to the window before settling back on Elizabeth. He cleared his throat. "Did Thornton's shop yield anything interesting?"

Elizabeth's fingers toyed with her teacup handle, her expression suddenly guarded.

A knowing smile tugged at Jonathan's lips. "That look speaks volumes. Perhaps it's you who is keeping secrets, Lady Elizabeth?"

She glanced away, then met his gaze with a sigh. "I suppose my visit wasn't entirely about shopping."

Jonathan leaned back, his eyebrow raised in silent question.

She cast a quick glance around the café. "Were you aware the police have ruled Mr Black's death a murder rather than an unfortunate accident?"

Jonathan's posture stiffened slightly. He nodded, his expression grave. "I heard they arrested young Tanner."

"Yes, the Chief Inspector seems determined to pin Mr Black's murder on Alfie because of some past grudge."

"And you believe he's innocent?"

"Of course." She nodded, her fingers tightening around her teacup. "The Tanners have worked on the Hawthorne estate for years. We've known Alfie since he was born. They're good, honest people."

"So why is the Chief Inspector so determined to blame the boy? Does he have any evidence?"

"The word of witnesses who apparently saw Alfie push Mr Black from his horse … but you were there. You saw how closely the horses were bunched, and I saw for myself how Mr Black was jostling and elbowing Alfie as they headed towards the final straight."

He leaned back in his chair, his fingers steepled. "Is there anything else? Any other evidence?"

"Some photographs from the local press, but the only thing they proved was how erratic Mr Black's horse was acting."

"Scant evidence indeed. So why is the Chief Inspector so intent on pursuing a conviction against the boy?"

Letting out a slow, frustrated breath, she recanted the tale of Mr Thornton's attack and Wainwright's simmering resentment over not being able to make the charges against Alfie stick.

"And since the scene of the alleged crime was practically next door to the police station, I thought I'd make some ... casual enquiries. To find out what really happened the night of Mr Thornton's attack," she added, her words measured.

Jonathan's lips curved into a knowing smile. "I suspected as much ... I knew there had to be an ulterior motive for the visit to Thornton's shop."

She set her teacup down, her gaze steady on Jonathan. "Now that I've revealed the true purpose of my visit to Thornton's, it's your turn to enlighten me on the reason for your covert surveillance."

Jonathan's fingers drummed against the table as his gaze flicked back to the window. His jaw tightened, betraying his internal struggle.

"Come now, Mr Ashcroft. Surely our previous collaborations have proved that I can be trusted?" Elizabeth straightened in her chair, her voice carrying a note of challenge.

"I've no concerns over your ability to maintain secrecy, Lady Elizabeth. It's your safety that worries me."

Elizabeth arched an eyebrow. "I can't imagine it's any more dangerous than being trapped in a blizzard with a foreign agent intent on taking down the government and a murderer, both of whom had been German collaborators during the war?"

Jonathan chuckled, his shoulders relaxing. "True," he conceded, shaking his head. "You do have a knack for finding yourself in some precarious situations."

"You sound just like my brother."

Jonathan's eyes crinkled at the corners at Elizabeth's comparison to her brother. He sighed, running a hand through his hair, dishevelling it slightly. The playful glint in his eyes faded, replaced by a flicker of uncertainty. He glanced around the café, then leaned in, his breath warm against her ear as he whispered, "I'm looking into a race-fixing ring."

The hairs on the back of Elizabeth's neck rose at Jonathan's proximity. She fought to keep her voice steady as she asked, "What do the Thorntons have to do with race fixing?"

His gaze flicked to the window, scanning the street outside before returning to Elizabeth. His voice was low. "I believe they're laundering money from the scam through their shop."

"From what I've heard about Sam Thornton, it wouldn't surprise me in the least if he was involved in shady dealings."

A muscle twitched beneath his skin. "Sam's a nasty piece of work, alright." His fingers drummed against the table, betraying his tension. "But I'm not sure whether Mr Thornton senior is involved or not."

Her mind flashed back to the burly man who'd entered the shop, his presence as incongruous as a cannon in a library. "What about that man who entered while I was there? The big fellow?"

Jonathan's eyes narrowed, his expression darkening. "He's some kind of henchman, as far as we can tell."

We? The word hung between them, unaddressed. She filed it away, another piece of the complex puzzle surrounding Jonathan Ashcroft. "Do you know who's in charge of this race-fixing scam?"

His lips momentarily thinned. "It's best if you don't know, Elizabeth. For your own safety."

She straightened, tilting her chin. Her gaze met his defiantly. "Surely, I'm the best judge of that, Mr Ashcroft. I'm hardly some wilting flower in need of a protector."

Jonathan's eyes darted around the café as if assessing the other patrons. "This goes far beyond a simple scam." He lowered his voice further before continuing. "We're talking about organised crime here, and I refuse to involve you any further, Lady Elizabeth."

Jonathan's gaze held hers, a rare vulnerability flickering across his features before he schooled his expression. "I think it would be wise if you steered clear of Thornton's ... at least for now."

"I appreciate your concern, Mr Ashcroft," she replied, her tone cool. "But I'm afraid I can't make such a promise. I must go wherever my investigation leads me."

She rose from her chair, smoothing her skirt. The weight of the Baby Browning in her bag was a comforting reminder of her self-reliance. "And I'd appreciate it if you didn't meddle in my investigations in the future under the pretext of rescuing me. I'm quite capable of handling myself."

Jonathan's eyebrow arched, a familiar glint of amusement in his eyes. "As you wish, Lady Elizabeth."

"Thank you for your insights, Mr Ashcroft." Elizabeth's lips pressed into a thin line as she placed a few coins on the table to cover her tea. She met Jonathan's gaze. "Now, if you'll excuse me, I'm expected at Rosewood Park."

The café's bell chimed as Elizabeth exited onto the busy street. Her conversation with Jonathan lingered in her thoughts as she made her way back to the police station. After settling into the soft leather upholstery of Iggy's motorcar, she gripped the steering wheel, taking a deep breath as the engine purred to life.

As she guided the Aston Martin along the winding country lanes back to Rosewood Park, her thoughts drifted to Jonathan Ashcroft.

She couldn't deny the thrill that ran through her whenever their paths crossed, the spark of excitement that ignited in her chest. Yet alongside it was a persistent unease. Jonathan was a riddle wrapped in an enigma. A puzzle Elizabeth wasn't sure she wanted to solve.

Who was Jonathan Ashcroft, really?

This question nagged at her since their very first encounter when he'd claimed to be an insurance underwriter. But Elizabeth had long suspected there was more to him than met the eye. His confidence, the air of quiet authority he exuded, the breadth of his connections –it all hinted at something … official.

Gripping the steering wheel, she tried to focus on the road ahead. But there was something about his earlier revelations that kept gnawing away at her.

Alfie, race fixing, money laundering – it all had one thing in common. Thornton's Pawnbrokers.

Her breath caught as if she'd been struck by a physical blow.

Had Alfie unwittingly managed to get himself mixed up in organised crime?

Chapter Thirteen

ELIZABETH SLIPPED INTO ROSEWOOD Park, her thoughts in a whirl. She'd just returned Iggy's Aston Martin to the garage, delayed by an unexpected encounter with Jonathan Ashcroft. The grandfather clock's chime reminded her how little time remained before dinner.

She hurried up the stairs, her mind still racing from the day's events. The visit to Alfie, the revelations at Thornton's, Jonathan's unexpected appearance and his worrying disclosures – so much had happened, and she needed time to process it all. But first, she had to change for dinner.

Meli turned from the vanity as she swept into the bedroom, a pearl-tipped pin hovering above her faux bob. "There you are! I was beginning to think you'd changed your mind and followed William and Caroline back to London."

"I was unexpectedly delayed," Elizabeth replied, her fingers working at the knot of her neck scarf as she crossed to the wardrobe.

Meli set down her hairpin. "Did that dreadful Chief Inspector finally allow you to see Alfie?"

Elizabeth nodded, reaching for a hanger. "He did."

"And?" Meli leaned forward, her half-finished hairstyle forgotten. "How was he?"

"I'll fill you in while I change," Elizabeth said, glancing at the clock. "We've precious little time before we're expected downstairs."

As Elizabeth recounted Alfie's version of the events on the night Mr Thornton was attacked, she pushed aside the hangers, her gaze settling on a midnight blue evening gown. Its beaded bodice caught the light, tiny crystals winking like stars against the inky silk. "Oh, Meli, you should have seen him. In that dreadful place, he looked ... he looked so terribly young."

Meli slid the final pearl-tipped pin into her faux bob, admiring the finished style in the mirror. "He's barely a year my junior. I can't even imagine how frightened he must be, with such a fate hanging over him."

Stepping behind the dressing screen, Elizabeth sighed. "He's trying to be brave, but his eyes ... they tell a different story. He swears he didn't push Mr Black, but Wainwright seems determined to pin it on him, no matter what."

She emerged from behind the screen, the gown's fringe a sparkling mist shimmering mid-calf. She stood beside the vanity, her fingers deftly fastening a delicate silver necklace at her throat. "After the station, I went straight to Thornton's shop. I'd hoped to speak with Mr Thornton about the night of the attack, to see if he'd managed to catch a glimpse of his assailant."

Meli paused, lipstick poised mid-application, and glanced up at Elizabeth. "Any luck?"

"Mr Thornton wasn't there, still recovering from his attack according to his son, Sam," Elizabeth replied, her gaze fixed on her reflection as she applied a touch of rouge. "A slippery fish, if ever I met one. He claimed Alfie was responsible for both the burglary and the attack on his father, although he didn't actually witness either." She paused, reaching for her mascara. "But he did let slip something rather intriguing."

Meli leaned forward, balancing precariously as she fastened the strap of her silver and pearl-beaded evening shoe. "Oh?"

"Apparently, Georgia provided Alfie's alibi for the time of the burglary. That's why the charges were dropped."

Meli's eyebrows shot up, her shoe forgotten. "How odd that Georgia never mentioned it this morning. You'd think she would have, given its importance."

"Indeed," Elizabeth murmured, scepticism colouring her tone. She tilted her head, dabbing perfume behind each ear with a delicate touch.

Meli straightened, her brow furrowed in thought. "Perhaps, given everything that's happened – Mr Black's fall, Alfie's arrest – it simply slipped her mind?"

"I suppose it's possible." Elizabeth reached for a silver hair comb on the vanity, slid it into place, and adjusted the sleek strands of her ebony bob.

Meli adjusted the swaying fringe on her dazzling coral flapper dress, its hemline daringly grazing her knees. "Did you manage to find out anything else?"

Elizabeth shook her head, draping a gossamer-thin midnight blue wrap over her shoulders. "My inquiry was cut short … by Mr Jonathan Ashcroft. He arrived just as I was questioning Sam Thornton."

A mischievous glint sparked in Meli's toffee-coloured eyes. "Ah, so that's why you're running late? An assignation with the mysterious Mr Ashcroft."

"Really, Meli, you have such a vivid imagination." She hesitated, Jonathan's unsettling revelations about money laundering and organised crime weighing on her mind. Deciding against sharing this information with her cousin, she swiftly changed tack. "How did your riding lesson with Georgia fare?"

Meli's hands fluttered excitedly as she spoke, her words tumbling out in a rush. "Oh, Elizabeth, it was simply marvellous! I can't believe I've never tried it before. Georgia is such a skilled horsewoman. I swear she's better than most men I've seen, and Rosewood's grounds?

Simply breathtaking. Did you know they have a lake?"

As Meli's animated account continued, Elizabeth listened attentively, inwardly relieved to have steered her cousin away from the topic of underworld crime.

The dinner gong rang out, silencing Meli mid-sentence. "Good heavens, we've missed the apéritifs altogether."

"Ready to face the music?" Elizabeth straightened, giving her reflection a final glance. The mirror showed a composed face, hiding the storm of thoughts beneath.

Elizabeth breezed into the dining room, Meli close behind. Her eyes swept the assembled guests. "Please forgive our lateness. It's entirely my–" The words caught in her throat as she spotted Jonathan Ashcroft, a hint of amusement in his expression. His presence was unexpected; he'd made no mention of dining at Rosewood Park when she'd seen him earlier. Then again, given the nature of their conversation and her hasty departure, there'd been little opportunity to discuss such social niceties as dinner plans.

Georgia's honeyed tones pierced Elizabeth's musings. "Don't fret, honey. We've only just begun." She motioned towards the vacant chairs, her diamond bracelet catching the light from the crystal chandelier overhead.

Elizabeth surveyed the two empty seats – one beside Enzo, the other next to Jonathan. She moved towards Enzo Bellini, keenly aware of Jonathan's gaze tracking her every step as Meli took her seat beside him.

"You already know Dolores, Cecil, and Enzo," Georgia said with a knowing smile. "Though Mr Ashcroft might be a new face. He's a friend of Enzo's."

"Mr Ashcroft and I are already acquainted," Elizabeth replied, her gaze meeting Jonathan's briefly across the table, but she volunteered no further details.

Georgia's eyebrows arched, a playful smile tugging at her lips. "My, my, Jonathan. Not holding out on us, are you?" She turned to him, mischief dancing in her eyes. "You sly old thing, you never mentioned you knew Elizabeth."

"They solved a murder together," Meli interjected, her words tumbling out in a rush.

"A murder?" Dolores echoed, her voice pitching higher as she lifted her glass. She took a generous sip before continuing, "Oh, you must mean one of those novels where everyone places bets on who'll guess the killer first. What's the author's name? Something Christie, isn't it?"

"Agatha Christie," Meli supplied, her admiration for the author unmistakable in her voice. "But no, Mrs Bentley, it was quite real, I assure you."

Cecil's muttered "Good Lord" was nearly lost in the gurgle of wine as a footman refilled his glass.

Enzo's gaze settled on Elizabeth, his dark eyes glinting with newfound interest. "Brains as well as beauty, Lady Elizabeth. It seems you are a woman of many talents."

"Isn't she just?" Georgia agreed, raising her glass in a gesture that appeared equal parts toast and challenge.

Eager to steer the conversation away from her alleged talents and her acquaintance with Jonathan Ashcroft, Elizabeth inclined her head towards the remaining empty chairs. "Will anyone else be dining with us this evening?"

Georgia's expression shifted, a hint of exasperation creeping in. "Amelia and Dominic were to join us, but they've cried off. Some drama or other," she said, meeting Dolores Bentley's eye roll with one of her own. The shared gesture spoke volumes about the frequency of such occurrences.

Cecil Bentley's lips thinned at the mention of their house guests. "There's always something with those two. I'll be glad when they leave so we can have some peace and quiet."

"You know what they say about fish and guests," Iggy remarked, reaching for his wine glass. He cast a sideways glance at his friend before subtly nodding towards Mr Bellini. "They both start to stink after a while."

The arrival of the first course brought a welcome distraction, its enticing aroma of truffle and wild mushroom soup wafting through the air. As conversation ebbed and flowed, Elizabeth observed the various undercurrents at play. Iggy's comment about fish and house guests seemed, on the surface, to target Cecil regarding Amelia and Dominic. But Elizabeth caught Iggy's sidelong glance at Enzo Bellini. The subtle dig surprised her; she had always known Iggy to be affable and easy-going, especially towards guests.

She recalled overhearing heated words between Iggy and Georgia about Enzo's frequent presence at Rosewood. Why did Georgia insist on having Enzo around so much, when it clearly bothered her husband?

"Lady Elizabeth," Enzo began, his tone light, fingers tapping the edge of his glass. "I'm curious – how does a woman like you get mixed up in something as grisly as murder?"

"It's a long story, I wouldn't want to bore you."

He leaned in slightly, his gaze playful. "Most women I meet are more concerned with securing marriage proposals than solving crimes."

"I am not most women, Mr Bellini, much to the frustration of my aunt, who believes my time would be better spent in pursuit of a husband."

Enzo chuckled, a rich, warm sound. "Ah, I can sympathise, Lady Elizabeth. My nonna back in Sicily is much the same. Every letter from her ends with a reminder that I'm not getting any younger and that she'd like to see great-grandchildren before she dies." His voice lowered conspiratorially. "Never mind that she's as strong as an ox and likely to outlive us all."

Although she laughed at Enzo's quip, a prickle of awareness ran down her spine. She resisted the urge to glance across the table, keeping her focus on her dinner companion. Yet the feeling lingered, an undercurrent beneath her smile.

As the last of the dessert plates were whisked away, Enzo cleared his throat. "I would like to make a toast," he said, drawing all eyes to him. "I'm pleased to announce that Lady Fairfax – Georgia – and I will soon be embarking on a new business venture here at Rosewood Park." He lifted his glass, turning slightly towards her. "To Georgia."

Elizabeth watched Georgia closely as the glasses were raised. Though a smile played on her lips, it faltered at the corners, never quite reaching her eyes. As she lifted her glass, a faint tremor passed through her hand. Her gaze flickered briefly towards Iggy before she quickly took a sip as if to steady herself.

From across the table, Elizabeth watched as Iggy's glass was quietly refilled, his grip tightening around the stem. He drank deeply, his gaze fixed firmly on the table, never once glancing in Georgia's direction. Elizabeth noted the way Georgia's smile faltered, her fingers gripping her glass a little too tightly. The air between them was thick with unspoken tension, though the other guests seemed oblivious, their laughter and chatter carrying on undisturbed. Georgia shifted in her seat, her eyes briefly flicking towards Iggy, but he didn't respond. Elizabeth could see the strain beneath her composed exterior.

Iggy's chair scraped against the floor. He gripped his cane, muscles tensing as he pushed himself to his feet with a slight wobble.

Georgia sprang up, her hand instinctively reaching out to steady him.

He yanked his arm away. "For God's sake, I'm not an invalid," he snapped, his words sharp enough to make Georgia flinch. "I can manage on my own."

Iggy turned, his cane striking the floor with each uneven step as he made his way to the door, leaving a heavy silence in his wake.

Chapter Fourteen

ELIZABETH EASED HER BEDROOM door shut, leaving Meli to her dreams. The exchange between Georgia and Iggy from the night before echoed in her mind, chasing away any hope of sleep.

The house was quiet as she made her way down the staircase. Despite the bright spring morning, the foyer felt gloomy, the dark wood panelling and heavy furniture seeming to absorb what little light filtered through the windows.

Pritchard materialised as if out of thin air, a plain envelope in his outstretched hand.

"My lady." Pritchard held out an envelope. "This was on the hall table first thing, but I'm afraid no one can account for its delivery."

Elizabeth took the envelope and ran her thumb over the unmarked paper. "How intriguing. Thank you, Pritchard."

Crisp morning air nipped at her cheeks the moment she stepped outside, early spring's chill still clinging to the grounds. Finding a secluded spot, she broke the seal and withdrew the contents.

Her breath hitched as her gaze landed on the name and contents. Reggie Black's post-mortem results.

She turned the envelope over in her hands, scanning it inside and out for any sign of where it had come from. But it revealed nothing.

Elizabeth unfolded the report and read, her eyes widening. The post-mortem revealed Reggie had been dead for several minutes before his fall, evidenced by the postural lividity distribution.

The pathologist's findings were equally startling: no bruising consistent with a fall, but a small puncture wound on the upper left thigh. More damning still, the toxicology report revealed a lethal concentration of morphine in his system.

The conclusion was as shocking as it was indisputable: Reggie Black had died from a lethal dose of morphine, not from his fall.

While this information could exonerate Alfie, Elizabeth knew she faced an uphill battle. Convincing the stubborn Chief Inspector Wainwright would take more than just this document.

If the real murderer was to be brought to justice, then she'd have to find them herself.

A flash of movement in the distance caught Elizabeth's eye. Georgia's copper curls whipped in the wind as she tore across the fields, her horse's hooves kicking up clods of earth with each powerful stride. Her fingers clenched around the paper as she watched Georgia charge towards the towering hedge.

"Surely she won't..." Elizabeth whispered, taking an involuntary step forward. The hedge loomed closer, its dense foliage an unyielding wall of green. Georgia leaned forward in the saddle, urging her mount on. Elizabeth's heart hammered against her ribs.

Then, at the last possible moment, the horse shied, veering sharply around the formidable obstacle. Elizabeth's shoulders sagged as the tension drained from her body, leaving her oddly light-headed.

She tucked the post-mortem report into the pocket of her skirt. She needed to speak with Georgia about the night Mr Thornton was attacked. The stables seemed the most obvious place to start, but as she rounded the corner, she found only Tommy, hunched over an injured horse.

"Nasty business, this," Tommy muttered, his eyes fixed on his work. His calloused hands moved with surprising gentleness as he filled a syringe from a small bottle.

Elizabeth stepped closer to the stall, her brow creasing. "What happened?"

Tommy's jaw tightened. "Strained tendon. Fool of a beast tried to take a jump it wasn't ready for." His words were harsh, but his gentle touch as he administered the injection betrayed his concern.

Elizabeth reached out and ran her hand along the horse's velvet muzzle. "How long until he's back on his feet?"

Tommy straightened, rolling his shoulders to ease the tension. "Days, if we're lucky." His gaze shifted to Elizabeth, eyes narrowing. "But I reckon you're not here about this one. How's the lad faring?"

Elizabeth's hand fell away from the horse, her fingers curling into a loose fist. "He's ... holding on. Scared, though he'd never admit it."

Tommy's lips pressed into a thin line, his expression grim. He busied himself with cleaning up the medical supplies. "Heard his lordship's hightailed it back to London."

"Some business he couldn't avoid, unfortunately," Elizabeth replied, her spine stiffening. She took a deep breath, forcing her voice to steady. "But I give you my word, neither of us will abandon Alfie."

The old trainer paused in his work, scepticism etched in every line of his weathered face. But Elizabeth met his gaze unflinchingly.

A moment passed, the silence broken only by the soft nickering of horses in nearby stalls. Elizabeth's hand brushed against the folded envelope in her pocket. "Tommy," she began, her voice low, "I couldn't help but notice some tension between Alfie and Mr Black. Do you know why they didn't get on?"

Tommy's hands stilled on the horse's flank. His shoulders sagged as if under an invisible weight. "He was so full of himself, that one," he muttered, not turning to face her. "He got on the wrong side of most people."

He paused, running a hand over his face before continuing. "Like his old trainer, Bucky. He was like a father to Reggie, then, soon as he started winning, he tossed Bucky aside like a worn-out saddle."

"Do you know where I might find this Bucky now?"

Tommy's laugh was harsh and humourless. "Here and there. Mostly at the bottom of a bottle, I'd wager." His eyes met Elizabeth's, a flicker of sympathy passing through them. "I give him work when I can, but…"

Elizabeth nodded, her fingers drumming lightly against the stall. "Can you think of anyone else?"

Tommy's lips twisted into a bitter smile. "Reggie fancied himself a ladies' man. Left a trail of broken hearts and angry menfolk in his wake."

He turned back to the horse. "I daresay there were more than a few who'd have paid good money to see him get what he deserved."

Tommy's words shed new light on Reggie's character. Elizabeth suspected Reggie and Amelia had been involved in an affair. If true, this cast Dominic Archer in an intriguing light. Perhaps he was amongst those willing to see Reggie *get what he deserved.*

"Thank you, Tommy. You've been most helpful."

Tommy nodded. "Glad I could be of service, m'lady."

As Elizabeth strode from the stables, she mulled over Mrs Bentley's gossip. Amelia Stanford's penchant for unsuitable men and Dominic Archer's reputation as a fortune hunter suddenly seemed far more significant.

She recalled the night at Rosewood Park – Dominic's fury as he'd struck Reggie, leaving him with a spectacular black eye.

Perhaps it was time she paid the Bentleys' houseguests a visit.

After collecting her coat and bag from the house, she slid into Iggy's Aston Martin and set off for the Bentleys'. The engine purred as she navigated the sweeping curves of their driveway, ancient oaks lining the path, their gnarled branches reaching skyward over the manicured lawns.

As she approached, the grand manor's understated elegance emerged. Ivy clung to its time-worn facade. Tall, mullioned windows gleamed, their slightly warped glass the only betrayal of time's passage.

Drawing to a stop before the broad front steps, she took in the scene, eyeing the neat flower beds framing the entrance. Two stone lions flanked the doorway, their fierce expressions unmarked by the years.

Exiting the car, she cradled a striking bouquet, hastily gathered from the gardens at Rosewood Park – an excuse, really, to justify her unannounced visit. She inhaled deeply, savouring the intoxicating blend of spring blooms – fragrant freesias, sweet peas, and early roses.

A cool breeze pricked at her cheeks as she climbed the front steps, bringing with it the unmistakable scent of approaching rain.

She rapped smartly on the weathered oak door. Moments later, it swung open, framing a butler in crisp attire that matched his precise manner. His eyes, sharp and assessing, swept over her before he offered a respectful nod.

"Good afternoon, madam. How may I assist you?"

"Good afternoon. I was hoping to speak with Mrs Bentley if she is at home."

"Of course, madam. Do come in." He stepped aside, revealing a spacious entrance hall. "May I have your name, please?"

"Lady Elizabeth Hawthorne."

The butler inclined his head slightly. "Thank you, Lady Elizabeth. Please, allow me a moment to enquire if Mrs Bentley is receiving visitors this afternoon."

Elizabeth waited in the entrance hall, a smile playing at her lips as she imagined Meli's reaction to the dark wood panelling and austere ancestral portraits. Her cousin would undoubtedly suggest replacing them all with some Étienne Laroche's for a much-needed splash of colour.

The butler appeared. "Mrs Bentley will see you now, Lady Elizabeth. If you'll kindly follow me."

She inclined her head. "Thank you."

He led her across the hall to the sitting room.

Dolores Bentley rose from her chair, her face brightening. "Lady Elizabeth! What a lovely surprise."

"These are for you, Mrs Bentley," Elizabeth said, offering the vibrant bouquet. "Freshly picked from the gardens at Rosewood Park." She cast a quick glance at Amelia, who'd barely managed a smile in greeting. "I recall you mentioning Miss Stanford was a little under the weather and thought these might lift her spirits."

Dolores accepted the flowers with delight, inhaling their fragrance. "Oh, how beautiful! They smell divine." She turned to Amelia, her voice softening. "Wasn't that thoughtful, Amelia?"

Amelia's gaze remained fixed on some distant point beyond the window, her lips barely twitching in response.

Dolores called over her shoulder, "Jenkins, would you bring us some tea?" She turned back to Elizabeth. "Is your cousin with you, my dear?"

Elizabeth shook her head as she settled into a plush armchair. "Meli has stayed behind at Rosewood Park. She has a riding lesson planned with Georgia."

A hint of amusement sparkled in Dolores's eyes. "I sometimes swear Georgia loves horses more than people."

"She certainly has a way with them."

Dolores glanced at the flowers. "If you'll excuse me, I must find a vase for these lovely blooms. We can't have them wilting, can we?" As she exited, Elizabeth caught a flicker of relief crossing the older woman's face, leaving her alone with the melancholic Amelia.

The maid brought in the tea tray and set it down quietly. Amelia didn't so much as acknowledge her, continuing to examine her perfectly manicured nails. Elizabeth thanked the girl, watching her retreat before turning expectantly to her companion. Amelia remained still, seemingly above such mundane tasks as pouring tea. Elizabeth felt a flicker of irritation at such blatant rudeness, both to the maid and to herself as a guest. Masking her disapproval, she reached for the teapot.

"Mr and Mrs Bentley's home is quite charming, isn't it?" Elizabeth asked, extending a cup towards her companion. "Do you visit often?"

Amelia accepted the cup, spooning three sugars into her tea. "Once or twice a year. Dolores is my mother's cousin. Since the passing of my parents, I suppose she's become something of a motherly figure to me." She paused, a spark of amusement dancing in her eyes. "Though I'm quite sure I'm a constant source of exasperation for both her and poor Cecil."

Elizabeth nodded, taking a sip of her own tea. It was almost as if Amelia took some kind of perverse pride in the distress her behaviour caused.

With the small talk soon exhausted, Elizabeth artfully broached the subject of Reggie's accident. "Wasn't it simply awful about Mr Black's fall? Such a tragedy."

"It's a dangerous sport," she mused, her voice level. "That's one of the things he loved about it, the thrill ... the rush when he crossed the finishing line." Her fingers found the rose-cut ruby on her left hand, twisting it absently. "Reggie likes ... liked to live on the edge."

Elizabeth set down her cup. "I heard whispers that Mr Black was considering stepping back from racing before his fall. Something about exploring new horizons?"

Amelia's lips twisted into a half-smile, her eyes glinting with amusement. "Reggie? Abandon the spotlight?" She let out a short, sharp laugh. "I'm afraid whoever told you that clearly didn't know him very well."

"I wondered if perhaps he was thinking of settling down," Elizabeth suggested, leaning forward slightly, her gaze fixed on Amelia's face.

Amelia drew back, her posture straightening as if a steel rod had been inserted along her spine. "I can assure you, Lady Elizabeth, domesticity was the furthest thing from Reggie's mind."

As she spoke, her thumb continued to work the ring around her finger, the movement at odds with the nonchalance she was trying to project.

Elizabeth's eyebrows arched, her head tilting to one side. "Oh? What makes you so certain?"

"Because Reggie's world revolved around one person, and one person only – Reggie Black."

Elizabeth paused, studying the minute shifts in Amelia's expression. "I suppose a family life and the demands of the racing world aren't exactly compatible, are they? Especially if what I've heard about the ... excesses is true." She lowered her voice. "I've heard whispers that some jockeys turn to certain ... stimulants to keep up with it all. To cope with the pressure."

Amelia's jaw clenched, a muscle twitching at her temple. She inhaled sharply and gripped the arm of her chair. "Reggie certainly liked to live on the edge," she replied. "But he never indulged in drugs." She set her teacup down with a soft clink. "He claimed they dulled the senses, and to stay at the top, you needed to keep your wits and your reflexes sharp."

Amelia crossed her legs, her fingers idly plucking at the hem of her dress where it rested on her knee. "You know, I used to tease Reggie about having a death wish. The risks he took on the track, the company he kept off it..." She shook her head, a rueful smile tugging at her lips. "But I never dreamed it would end like this. I thought..." Her voice softened, a hint of wistfulness creeping in. "I suppose I thought we had more time."

Amelia's wistful tone solidified Elizabeth's suspicions, hinting at more than a casual acquaintance between her and Reggie. She pondered the jockey's reputation as a ladies' man, but Amelia's comment about *the company he kept off the track* nagged at her. What company had he been keeping that could have potentially threatened his life?

She weighed her next move carefully. Amelia's relationship with Dominic Archer could prove crucial to understanding the dynamics at play. She kept her voice light but probing. "And what of your own romantic prospects, Miss Stanford? Might we soon hear wedding bells for you and Mr Archer?"

Amelia's eyebrows shot up, a hint of amusement curling at the corners of her mouth. "With Dominic? Hardly." She shook her head, a touch of ruefulness in her smile. "He's handsome and charming, I'll give him that," she added, her tone taking on a knowing edge. "But I've already walked the matrimonial path twice with men more interested in my bank balance than me. I won't be making that mistake again."

Dolores slipped back into the room. "Oh, I'm terribly sorry," she said, smoothing her hair. "Cook needed my urgent attention … You know how it is." Her eyes darted between Elizabeth and Amelia. "Shall I ring for fresh tea?"

Elizabeth rose. "Thank you, but I really must be getting back to Rosewood. Perhaps another time."

"Of course, my dear," Dolores murmured, her lips thinning as she flicked her gaze to Amelia. "Although you're more than welcome to stay."

Elizabeth shook her head. "Thank you, but I really must go. I've imposed on your hospitality long enough."

Dolores reached for the bell pull. The soft chime echoed through the house, and Jenkins appeared in the doorway.

"Lady Elizabeth is leaving," Dolores announced. "See her out, will you?"

Amelia remained seated, her attention seemingly caught by the first drops of rain hitting the window.

The rain intensified as Elizabeth emerged from the Bentleys. The graphite sky made good on its earlier promise as fat droplets pelted the gravel drive. She raced towards Iggy's Aston Martin and slid into the driver's seat just as the heavens opened.

She eased Iggy's motorcar around yet another bend, its engine purring even at this crawling pace. Her knuckles whitened as her grip intensified on the steering wheel. Rain pelted the windscreen with relentless fury, and the wipers worked overtime, barely keeping up with the deluge. Squinting through the grey curtain of water, she struggled to make out the twists and turns of the country lane.

Up ahead, a lone figure huddled beneath the sprawling branches of an ancient oak. She squinted as she drew nearer, the silhouette sharpening into the familiar form of Dominic Archer, his shoulders hunched against the downpour.

She eased off the accelerator, bringing the car to a halt in front of him. Sliding down the window, she called out, "Mr Archer! Would you care for a lift?"

Dominic glanced up, raindrops clinging to his dark lashes. "Thank you, Lady Elizabeth, but I'm sure it will pass soon enough."

"Come now, Mr Archer," she urged, feeling the cool mist of rain on her cheek. "Come inside and dry off. You'll catch your death out there."

For a moment, he hesitated. Then, with a resigned nod, he yanked open the door and slid into the passenger seat.

"I've just come from the Bentleys'," Elizabeth said, breaking the silence that had settled between them. "They're such a charming couple, aren't they?"

Dominic shifted uncomfortably, his gaze fixed on the rain-lashed windscreen. "I suppose."

The steady drumming of rain on the car's roof filled the silence. Elizabeth's gaze flicked to Dominic before she spoke. "Such a tragedy about Mr Black's accident, don't you think?"

Dominic's jaw tightened. "He knew the risks."

She chose her words carefully, deliberately including mention of Amelia in her question. "Did you and Miss Stanford know him well?"

A muscle twitched in Dominic's cheek. "Not as well as Amelia seemed to," he replied, his narrowed gaze still fixed on the rain-lashed windscreen.

Dominic's fingers curled into fists, his knuckles whitening against the dark fabric of his trousers.

"Reggie Black was a cad," he spat suddenly, the words bursting from him like a dam breaking. "He got what he deserved."

Elizabeth's eyebrows arched, her lips parting in surprise. This passionate outburst was a far cry from Dominic's earlier clipped responses.

He dragged a hand through his damp hair, leaving it standing in dishevelled spikes. "I ... I shouldn't–" He broke off, shaking his head. When he turned to face Elizabeth, his eyes blazed with an intensity that caught her off guard. "I know what they say about me. That I'm only after Amelia's money. But it's not true." His voice dropped, raw with emotion. "I love her. I would do anything for her."

She leaned back slightly, her eyes widening at Dominic's unexpected outburst.

His gaze flicked to the window, where the rain had slackened to a gentle patter against the glass.

"I should go," he said abruptly, his hand already on the door handle. "Thank you for the shelter."

Elizabeth watched him go, his passionate declaration lingering in the empty space beside her.

I would do anything for her. The words tumbled through her mind, each repetition unveiling new, unsettling possibilities. Her fingers tightened on the steering wheel, her knuckles blanching as she grappled with the implications of Dominic's admission.

Had Dominic Archer murdered Reggie Black?

And if he was the killer, had his motive been love … or jealousy?

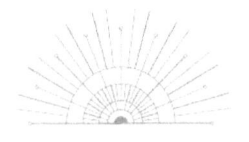

Chapter Fifteen

ELIZABETH CROSSED THE THRESHOLD of Rosewood Park, fatigue settling into her bones. The day had been a whirlwind – her visit to the Bentleys, a conversation with Amelia, and the unexpected encounter with Dominic Archer. All she wanted now was a hot bath and the comfort of an early night.

"There you are!" Meli appeared in the doorway, a book clutched in her hand. "I've been looking for you all day," she said, crossing to where Elizabeth stood.

"I'm so sorry, Meli," Elizabeth replied, setting down her handbag. "Didn't you get my message? I left word with Iggy when I collected the motorcar keys."

Meli shook her head. "Pritchard mentioned you'd gone to visit the Bentleys, but I haven't seen Iggy all today. How was he?"

"Apologetic. How was your riding lesson with Georgia?" she asked, hanging up her coat.

Meli shrugged. "It was fine, but Georgia cut it short when Mr Bellini arrived. Said they had some business to take care of."

Elizabeth's eyebrows rose. "Mr Bellini was here?" Enzo Bellini back at Rosewood Park, after last night's upset – it didn't make sense. Why on earth would Georgia agree to his presence, knowing how Iggy felt about him?

"He was." Meli nodded. "And he seemed disappointed you weren't here. I'd say he's quite taken with you. He's invited us all to his club tonight. I hope you don't mind, but I've already accepted."

The urge to retreat to a quiet evening pulled at Elizabeth, but Meli's enthusiasm was making it difficult to refuse.

"It's just ... it's so frightfully dull here. I know we have to stay until Alfie's released," she quickly added. "But..."

Elizabeth felt a pang of guilt. They'd only meant to stay a few days for the Grand National, but Alfie's arrest and William's sudden recall to London had extended their visit indefinitely. And she had left Meli alone all day.

"Very well," she conceded.

Meli's face lit up. "Wonderful! I've already picked out my outfit."

Looping her arm through Elizabeth's, Meli led her up the stairs towards their bedroom.

"What took you to the Bentleys' today?" Meli asked the moment they were inside. "I'd have jumped at the chance to join you – anything to escape the monotony here."

"I hadn't planned on going there, but one thing led to another, and before I knew it, the day had gotten away from me."

"How do you mean?"

She reached into her pocket and handed Meli the envelope.

Meli's eyes widened as she scanned the document. "The post-mortem results? Where did you get this?"

Elizabeth leaned against the wardrobe, her arms crossed. "That's the oddest thing.

Pritchard gave it to me this morning, but no one seems to know where it came from."

"Do you think William sent it? Or the Chief Inspector?" Meli perched on the edge of her bed, still clutching the paper.

"If William had arranged for a copy, he would have telephoned," Elizabeth replied, shaking her head. "And I highly doubt the Chief Inspector would have provided this information, especially since it proves Mr Black was already dead before he fell."

Meli sat up straighter, her eyes darting back to the document. "But if Mr Black was already dead before he fell … even if Alfie had pushed him, he didn't kill him. Surely this means that mean old Chief Inspector will have to release him?"

Elizabeth pushed away from the wardrobe, pacing the length of the room. "I wish it were that simple. But Wainwright's grudge against Alfie runs so deep he'll likely twist this, claim Alfie could have administered the injection during the race or some such nonsense."

A heavy silence fell between them. Elizabeth's gaze drifted to the window, her reflection pale against the darkening sky.

"What is it?" Meli asked softly.

Elizabeth turned, her eyes meeting Meli's. "I … I saw Alfie, just before the race. He was arguing with Reggie. I recognised their rather distinctive riding silks."

Meli's hand flew to her mouth. "Surely, you don't think Alfie was responsible for injecting Reggie, do you?"

"No, of course not," Elizabeth said firmly, but her voice wavered slightly. She sank onto the edge of her bed. "But it doesn't look good, does it?"

Meli sat beside her. "What do you think he was doing there?"

Elizabeth shook her head. "I don't know, but as he was fleeing, he knocked over one of the racing easels, drawing the attention of others."

"And if the inspector finds out…" Meli's voice trailed off.

"Exactly," Elizabeth replied, straightening. "Which means I need to find the real killer before the Chief Inspector discovers this information."

"I still don't see how this connects to the Bentleys."

Elizabeth paused at the wardrobe, her gaze flitting between a burgundy gown and an emerald silk number. She chose the latter, its Art Deco-inspired beadwork catching the electric light. "It's rather a roundabout tale. Tommy's remark about Mr Black led me to the Bentleys."

As they dressed, Elizabeth recounted her visit, noting how she'd gleaned information from Amelia's demeanour and unspoken cues. Meli listened keenly, donning a pale pink chiffon dress with a dropped waist, its hem swaying just below her knees.

Elizabeth reached for her mascara. "But it was Mr Archer's declaration of love that truly caught me off guard."

Meli secured the T-strap on her silver dancing shoes. "Elizabeth, might Mr Archer be involved in Mr Black's death, do you think?"

She paused, lipstick hovering near her lips as she pondered. "It's conceivable. He certainly has compelling motives: love and jealousy."

"A perilous combination indeed," Meli murmured.

The clock struck the hour, its chime reminding them of the time.

"Hurry, Elizabeth! We're going to be late, and I'll simply die if I don't escape this gloomy old prison soon and have some fun."

"Don't be so melodramatic." Elizabeth's lips twitched, fighting a smile as she shook her head at her cousin's theatrics.

Meli's excitement was infectious, and despite herself, Elizabeth felt a spark of anticipation for the evening ahead as they made their way downstairs to join the others.

Georgia met them at the foot of the stairs. She wore a striking gold gown, her auburn hair swept up in an elegant chignon. "There you are! I thought perhaps you'd changed your minds."

"Not a chance," Meli responded.

Elizabeth glanced around the foyer. "Will Iggy be joining us?"

Georgia's smile faltered for a fraction of a second, a shadow passing behind her eyes. "Er, no ... it's not really his kind of thing."

"Nothing ever is anymore." Her voice was low, tinged with bitterness.

Elizabeth blinked, unsure if she'd heard correctly. "I'm sorry, what was that?"

Georgia whirled back, her smile firmly in place once more. "Just thinking aloud, honey." She clapped her hands together. "Now, are you ladies ready? We don't want to miss all the fun, do we?"

Georgia led the way outside to where Simmons was waiting.

The country lanes soon gave way to Liverpool's cityscape. Gas lamps cast pools of light on cobblestones as they neared the docks.

The motorcar slowed and stopped before an unassuming door. They emerged into the night air. A nod from the doorman, and they stepped into another world.

The sultry notes of a jazz saxophone wove through the chatter of Adelina's patrons. A peal of laughter erupted from a corner booth, drawing curious glances. Cigarette smoke hung in lazy curls beneath the electric sconces, their light catching on crystal decanters and the gleaming brass rail of the mahogany bar.

As Elizabeth, Meli, and Georgia neared the central table, a hostess approached them. "Good evening, Lady Fairfax, such a pleasure to see you again. Mr Bellini's expecting you."

Elizabeth navigated the maze of tables encircling Adelina's dance floor. Couples swayed to the jazz band's sultry rhythm, their movements a mesmerising ebb and flow. As they ventured further, the club's atmosphere shifted. Tables sprawled further apart, revealing plush velvet booths. Diamonds glinted on wrists and necks, catching the glow of crystal chandeliers. Hushed voices replaced boisterous laughter, secrets traded over champagne flutes. They'd crossed an invisible threshold into Adelina's inner sanctum, where privilege and discretion intertwined.

Enzo Bellini commanded attention at the centre of a crowded table. Conversation died as the ladies approached, curious gazes tracking their every move. Enzo unfolded from his seat, his tailored suit accentuating his height. His smile, sharp as a razor's edge, flashed in the dim light.

"Georgia, fashionably late as always."

"It's the only way to make an entrance, honey."

Enzo's gaze slid to Elizabeth, lingering a heartbeat too long. He lifted her gloved hand to his lips. "Lady Elizabeth, a pleasure as always."

His smile softened as he turned to Meli. "Miss Diomaros, I'm delighted you could join us this evening."

Enzo made swift introductions, his hand gesturing to each guest in turn. "I believe you already know everyone, Georgia."

He turned to Elizabeth, his voice lowering. "I've saved you a seat, Lady Elizabeth. Right here." He gestured to the chair beside him.

Georgia slipped into a seat across from them, already deep in conversation with a dashing young man and a stunning brunette.

Elizabeth settled next to Enzo, Meli on her other side. Champagne fizzed into crystal flutes as the jazz band struck up a lively tune, conversation rising to meet it.

"Lady Elizabeth, I understand you drive a Duesenberg."

Elizabeth leaned back, her eyes narrowing slightly. "How on earth do you know that?" She couldn't tell if she should feel flattered or concerned.

"Let's just say I have my sources." Enzo's eyes glinted. "But you know, I'm convinced that if you tried a *Fraschini*, you'll never look at your American motorcar the same way again."

"Oh? What makes you so certain?"

"Because Italians do everything better," he said with a confident smile. "Allow me to take you out and prove it to you."

"That sounds like quite the challenge, Mr Bellini."

"Well, I've heard you're not one to shy away from a challenge, Lady Elizabeth."

She paused, considering his words. "While intriguing, I'm afraid my schedule leaves little room for such diversions at present."

"I'm a patient man," he countered, his gaze unwavering. "I can wait."

The opening notes of "Black Bottom" filled the air. A young man approached, his eyes locked on Meli. "Miss Diomaros, would you care to dance?"

Enzo's eyebrows furrowed as he addressed his cousin, his voice holding a warning tone.

"Antonio, comportati bene. Porta rispetto alla signorina."

Antonio's eyes widened in mock offense, his hand dramatically placed over his heart. *"Ma cugino, non lo faccio sempre?"*

Satisfied, Enzo turned to Elizabeth. "My younger cousin, Antonio. He's a good boy. He'll treat Miss Diomaros with the proper respect … or he'll answer to me."

Elizabeth tilted her head slightly. "I'm sure he will, Mr Bellini."

As "Black Bottom" pulsed through the club, Elizabeth's focus shifted to the man approaching – a Mediterranean figure in a perfectly tailored suit, his stern expression out of place in the lively scene. Enzo's smile faded instantly, his playful demeanour giving way to tense restraint.

The newcomer leaned in and whispered rapid Italian in Enzo's ear. Elizabeth couldn't grasp the words, but Enzo's body spoke volumes. His shoulders stiffened, jaw set tight, responding only with sharp nods. Whatever the message, it wasn't good.

Enzo's fingers drummed a rapid rhythm on the tablecloth as he turned to Elizabeth, his expression tightening. "Lady Elizabeth, I–" He paused, sighing. "I must apologise. An urgent matter requires my immediate attention." He signalled to a passing waiter. "Please, order whatever you'd like. I'll return as soon as I can."

He disappeared into the crowd, still engaged in hushed conversation with the suited man. Her gaze swept across Adelina's interior. Sleek chrome fixtures and polished Art Deco mirrors lined the walls, their surfaces catching the cool blue haze of cigarette smoke and the glint of shimmering sequins. Along the walls, low-slung leather banquettes housed intimate gatherings, their occupants leaning close, voices inaudible against the lively backdrop.

A flicker of movement in the far corner caught her eye. She blinked, focusing on what appeared to be a shimmering patch of wall. No, not the wall – a curtain, its rich velvet matching the wallpaper perfectly. As she watched, a gentleman in evening dress slipped behind it, the fabric settling without a sound.

Intrigued, Elizabeth straightened, her attention fixed on that corner. Over the next few minutes, she observed other patrons approach the same spot. A silver-haired gentleman paused to light a cigar before disappearing. A younger man tugged at his collar, glancing around before he too vanished behind the curtain. Each moved with practiced ease, suggesting a familiarity.

The music swelled, pulling Elizabeth from her observations. She rose, the beads on her gown catching the light as she moved. Her gaze swept towards the dance floor where Meli twirled amidst the energetic strains of "Ain't We Got Fun". With a final look at Enzo's retreating form, now barely visible in the crowd, she wove between the tables as she crossed the room, her eyes periodically flicking towards the far corner where the curtain rippled.

She lingered before an Etienne Laroche painting, its bold colours and abstract forms a striking shift from Adelina's understated elegance. As she moved to the next piece, her gaze slid to the nearby curtain. The shallow recess behind it finally explained the patrons' baffling disappearances.

Elizabeth angled herself for a better view, feigning interest in another of the artwork as a gentleman approached the curtain. He slipped behind the velvet folds, vanishing entirely from sight. A moment later, a series of knocks sounded: two rapid, a pause, then three more.

She watched as others repeated the ritual. Her eyes narrowed as she made the connection – each patron wore a small silver pin with a polished A. The pin wasn't mere decoration; it was a key to whatever lay beyond that curtain.

Committing every detail to memory, Elizabeth bided her time. Her chance arrived as a man lurched out from behind the curtain, unsteady on his feet. Stepping into his path, she let out a soft gasp as they collided. "Oh, I do beg your pardon," she murmured, one hand steadying him while the other deftly plucked the pin from his lapel.

"No harm done, m'dear," he slurred, tottering away, oblivious to the theft.

She fastened the pin to her dress and scanned the room. Certain no one was watching, she slipped behind the curtain, disappearing into the shadows.

She raised her hand and knocked: two quick, a pause, three more. The hatch opened. Dark eyes met hers, then dropped to the silver pin as the door groaned open.

Anticipation twisted with uncertainty as her heart pounded. Whatever awaited beyond the door, it was too late to turn back now.

Chapter Sixteen

Smoke and secrets. Elizabeth inhaled both as she slipped into Adelina's inner sanctum. The jazz faded, replaced by the rustle of cards and the low murmur of hushed wagers.

Men in evening dress hunched over green baize, their faces obscured by curling tendrils of cigar smoke. While women draped in silk and jewels watched with calculated interest. Chips clicked and cards snapped, a steady rhythm punctuated by sharp intakes of breath and muttered curses.

Elizabeth's gaze darted from face to face, searching for any sign of Enzo Bellini. A waiter glided past, crystal glasses tinkling on his silver tray. She snagged a flute of champagne and used it to mask her scrutiny of this inner sanctum.

A statuesque hostess with raven hair approached, her smile warm but her dark eyes scanning Elizabeth's attire with familiar ease, her gaze lingering on the silver pin. "Good evening, madam. Welcome to Adelina's," she said, her voice as smooth as the silk of her black cocktail gown. "I don't believe I've seen you here before. Is this your first visit?"

Elizabeth's fingers tightened around her champagne flute. "Yes, it is. I'm visiting friends in the area."

The hostess's smile widened, but her eyes remained cold. "Might I be so bold as to enquire who ... so that I can thank them."

Elizabeth opened her mouth, then closed it again, her mind blank. The hostess's eyes narrowed slightly, her head tilting to one side.

"Lady Elizabeth!" A familiar voice cut through the tension like a knife. "What a surprise."

Amelia Stanford swept across the room, her crimson gown swirling around her feet. She air-kissed Elizabeth's cheek, the scent of alcohol pungent on her breath. "No need to interrogate the poor woman," she snapped at the hostess, waving a bejewelled hand.

The woman's posture stiffened, her smile frozen. "Of course, Miss Stanford." With a slight bow, she retreated into the crowd.

Amelia's gaze flicked to Elizabeth's lapel, her perfectly shaped eyebrow arching. "Aren't you a dark horse, Lady Elizabeth. I never thought I'd see you in a place like this."

Elizabeth's chin lifted slightly. "Oh? And why is that?"

Amelia's laugh tinkled like ice in a glass as she snagged a fresh champagne flute from a passing waiter. "Oh, you know..." She paused to take a sip before continuing. "I suppose I thought you were a bit ... proper. All rules and no fun."

As she spoke, her eyes scanned the room with the ease of familiarity, nodding to a few patrons across the way.

"While this may be my first time at Adelina's," Elizabeth replied with an easy smile designed to put Amelia at ease, "I'm not entirely unfamiliar with establishments such as Adelina's."

Surprise flickered in Amelia's eyes. She glanced around the room again, this time with more purpose. "I suppose Calamity Jane is with you?"

Calamity Jane? Did she mean Georgia? Was Georgia a member of the clandestine gambling establishment? She took a quick sip of champagne to hide her confusion. "She's in the main club."

A shadow passed over Amelia's face, her lip curling slightly. "No doubt she'll honour us with her presence before the night is out."

Elizabeth's eyebrows rose slightly at the bitterness in Amelia's voice. Clearly there was no love lost there, but the question was why.

Elizabeth glanced around, her curiosity getting the better of her. "Is Mr Archer not with you this evening?"

Amelia's face darkened. "Dominic? No, he's become such a bore, so clingy. I simply had to get away."

Her mood shifted suddenly, excitement flaring in her eyes. "Elizabeth, come, the tables are calling our names." Without waiting for a response, she linked her arm through Elizabeth's, steering them both through the crowd.

They approached a long, green-felted table surrounded by a boisterous group. Amelia elbowed her way to the front, dragging Elizabeth alongside her.

The crowd parted, revealing a game in progress. Two ivory dice clattered across the table, coming to rest against the far wall. A cheer went up from half the onlookers, while others groaned in disappointment.

"Isn't it thrilling?" Amelia gushed, her eyes bright. "It's called Craps – straight from the States. It's deliciously unpredictable."

Elizabeth watched as Amelia plucked a handful of high-value chips from her purse and tossed them onto the table.

"Place your bets, ladies and gentlemen!" the croupier called out.

"The trick is to bet big and bet often." Amelia's gaze lingered on the handsome gentleman beside her, who tipped his glass with a knowing smile.

The dice passed to the next shooter, and Elizabeth felt the electric charge in the air. Tension and excitement crackled around her, building with each of Amelia's escalating cries. The crowd pressed closer, their collective breath held in anticipation.

"You simply must have a go," Amelia urged, her eyes sparkling as she pressed a stack of chips into Elizabeth's hand. "One little wager and you'll be hooked. It's positively exhilarating."

Elizabeth hesitated, the weight of the chips heavy in her palm. She glanced around the table, noting the flushed faces and fevered eyes of the other players. Was this really the best use of her time? But then again, perhaps it would help her get to the bottom of Amelia's antipathy towards Georgia. Deciding to play along for now, she took a deep breath and placed a bet.

As the dice rolled, she turned to Amelia. "I'm curious … why do you call Georgia *Calamity Jane*?"

Amelia snorted, her eyes fixed on the tumbling dice. "Oh, you know. She's just so … American. All rough and ready, like she's fresh off the stagecoach." She took a long drink of champagne. "I simply can't fathom what Reggie saw in her."

Elizabeth froze, her mind reeling. "Reggie? You mean Reggie Black?"

The dice clattered to a stop, but Elizabeth barely registered the cheers erupting around them. She stared at Amelia, stunned by the revelation.

Georgia and Reggie?

It seemed impossible, and yet...

Amelia's words rang in her ears, drowning out the dice clatter and excited shouts around her.

"Feeling lucky, Lady Elizabeth?"

His voice cut into her thoughts, momentarily displacing the shock of Amelia's revelation. She inhaled sharply, quickly schooling her features to mask the jumble of emotions he always seemed to stir within her.

She turned, arching an eyebrow as she met his gaze. "Mr Ashcroft. What an unexpected pleasure."

"The pleasure, as always, is mine." The initial warmth in Jonathan's eyes cooled as his gaze settled on the silver pin on her shoulder. "I wouldn't have had you pegged as a member of Adelina's ... exclusive little club?"

"Perhaps you don't know me as well as you thought." She met Jonathan's eyes, her own gaze steady and unblinking. "And what of your presence, Mr Ashcroft–"

"I love this game!" Amelia practically vibrated as the croupier pushed a stack of chips towards her. "Mr Ashcroft, how marvellous to see you again. I insist you take a turn. It's so exhilarating."

"Lady Luck does indeed seem to be favouring you tonight, Miss Stanford, but another time perhaps," Jonathan said smoothly. He turned to Amelia. "Might I borrow Lady Elizabeth for a moment? We have some catching up to do."

Amelia's eyes flicked between them, noting the small gap between Jonathan and Elizabeth. She inclined her head, a sly smile curving her lips. "Please," she purred, swirling her champagne. "Enjoy your little ... catch-up."

Jonathan guided Elizabeth to a quieter corner, his grip on her elbow loosening as they stopped. His voice dropped low, urgent. "What are you doing here, Elizabeth?"

Elizabeth met his gaze squarely. "I could ask you the same question." As the words left her lips, the pieces clicked into place. Jonathan's earlier mention of race-fixing, his unexpected presence here in Bellini's den – it was all connected. She leaned in, her voice low. "This isn't about poker, is it? You're here because of Bellini."

Jonathan's casual demeanour slipped for a moment before he caught himself. "Elizabeth–"

"The race-fixing scandal," she pressed, watching his reaction closely. "That's why you're really here, isn't it?"

Jonathan straightened, closing the distance between them. His voice dropped to an urgent whisper. "Elizabeth, listen to me. You need to stay away from Enzo Bellini. He's not who you think he is. He's–"

The words died on his lips as his gaze snapped to the far end of the room. Elizabeth followed his line of sight, noticing a panel in the wall sliding open. A figure emerged, silhouetted against the light from beyond.

Jonathan's hand found the small of her back, urging her to move. "We need to leave. Now," he murmured, his lips barely moving.

Elizabeth threw a last glance over her shoulder as they neared the exit. The silhouetted figure was now visible. Enzo Bellini surveyed the room, his dark eyes sweeping across his domain. For a heart-stopping moment, his gaze seemed to lock with hers before Jonathan pulled her through the doorway, and Bellini vanished from view.

Slipping back through the velvet curtain, Jonathan led Elizabeth straight to the dance floor just as the band struck up a lively Charleston. His hand settled at her waist as they fell into step with the other couples.

He leaned close, his breath warm against her ear. "We need something to explain your absence."

Elizabeth tilted her head, her eyes questioning.

"Dancing. The perfect alibi for your disappearance."

Sequins flashed under the electric light as dancers kicked and twisted. Elizabeth mirrored

Jonathan's every move, their steps sharp and synchronised. The music swelled, offering a veil of privacy.

"Enzo Bellini isn't who you think he is, Elizabeth." His breath hitched. "You'd do well to keep your distance."

Her eyes narrowed. "Is that all you're going to tell me?"

"Trust me. The less you know, the better."

She wanted to trust him – heaven knows, she did. There was something about Jonathan that drew her in, a depth of character that intrigued her. But how could she fully trust someone who seemed to exist in a world of half-truths and carefully crafted personas?

His unexpected appearances, always accompanied by plausible yet vague explanations, puzzled her. His connections spanned from high society to the criminal underworld, but he never revealed how he navigated these spheres.

Their encounters both fascinated and frustrated her. His quick wit and charm drew her in, while his evasiveness pushed her away.

She searched his face for any chink in his armour.

Finding none, she took a breath, steering the conversation away from Mr Bellini and his dubious business dealings and back to the more pressing concern of Alfie's incarceration. "Perhaps you're right, Mr Ashcroft, and a change of subject is in order." She paused as if adding weight to her comment. "Do you know if Mr Black was a regular here?"

Jonathan's eyes flickered briefly towards the velvet curtain. "Mr Black was a regular wherever the stakes were high. Adelina's was just one of many."

"What do you mean?"

Jonathan's gaze swept the room before returning to her. "Word is, Reggie Black lost more often than he won and owed money all over town."

"Including Enzo Bellini?"

"Among others."

Her thoughts churned, each new revelation adding another piece to an increasingly complex puzzle. Bellini's shadowy connections, Adelina's clandestine gambling den, Reggie's spiralling debts – how did they all fit together? And lurking at the heart of it all, could Enzo Bellini be the orchestrator of Reggie Black's death?

"I wonder what other secrets Reggie took to his grave."

Jonathan leaned in closer, his lips nearly brushing her ear. "Secrets have a way of leaving traces ... marks, even, if one knows where to look."

Elizabeth's eyes widened. "That's ... rather specific, Mr Ashcroft."

"Is it? In my experience, the devil often lurks in such details. Especially when appearances deceive."

Elizabeth's mind raced. How could Jonathan know about the marks mentioned in the post-mortem report? Unless ... he was the one who'd left it for her?

The lively rhythm faded, replaced by the low hum of conversation. Elizabeth felt Jonathan stiffen beside her, his gaze fixed on a point across the room. She turned, her breath catching as she spotted Enzo and his suited companion emerging from behind the velvet curtain.

Her gaze snapped back to Jonathan. "I think he saw me … in the gambling den."

Jonathan's mask slipped, just for a heartbeat but long enough to betray his concern. "Just act natural," he said, his eyes darting towards Enzo's table. "We'll return to the others as if nothing is amiss."

They wove through the crowd, each step deliberate and unhurried. "Bellini is not a man to be crossed," Jonathan whispered, his lips barely moving as Enzo's table loomed closer. "Keep away from him, Elizabeth."

Enzo rose as they approached, all easy smiles and polished charm. "Lady Elizabeth, I must apologise for my prolonged absence, but I see you found other ways to amuse yourself." His gaze slid to Jonathan, a hint of challenge in his tone. "Ashcroft, you managed to keep hold of your shirt tonight. Perhaps fortune was on your side … this time?"

Enzo's gaze lingered on her as she reclaimed her seat. "Lady Elizabeth, that outing we discussed, when can we arrange it for? I'm eager to pit my Isotta Fraschini against your Duesenberg."

'Bellini is not a man to be crossed' Jonathan's words echoed in her mind. Jonathan wasn't a man for fanciful exaggerations in her experience, so she had no reason to doubt his words.

But what if Bellini was indeed the man responsible for Reggie's death? Could she pass up this opportunity to gather evidence that might exonerate Alfie?

"That sounds very much like a challenge, Mr Bellini … and I do love a challenge."

"Excellent." Enzo's lips curled into a self-satisfied smile, his gaze flicking briefly towards Jonathan. "And please, my friends call me Enzo."

Elizabeth met Enzo's gaze, her lips curving into an inviting smile as she pointedly ignored the weight of Jonathan's glare. "In that case, you must call me Elizabeth."

Chapter Seventeen

ELIZABETH STOOD AT THE bedroom window, her gaze sweeping the neatly trimmed lawns and rose garden beyond, where crimson and pink blooms nodded in the morning breeze. The events of the previous night at Adelina's occupied her thoughts – a tangle of revelations and questions that demanded answers. Amelia's startling comments about Georgia and Reggie, Jonathan's warnings about Enzo Bellini, and Bellini's calculated charm all vied for her attention.

"I'm not surprised Georgia missed breakfast," Meli remarked, stifling a yawn as she stretched her arms above her head. "I lost count of how many gin rickeys she had."

Elizabeth turned from the window, her brow knitted as she mulled over the previous night's events. She recalled Georgia's increasingly boisterous laughter as the night wore on, the way her cheeks had flushed a deeper shade of pink with each passing hour. "Indeed. Though I must say, Iggy didn't seem quite himself this morning. He barely touched his breakfast."

Meli lowered her arms, her expression turning serious as she caught Elizabeth's reflection in the mirror. "Elizabeth, do you think he was upset about Georgia's condition when we returned last night?"

"I thought he seemed more preoccupied than upset. As if something else was bothering him."

"Do you think there could be any truth to what Miss Stanford said? About Georgia and Reggie?" Meli asked. "Georgia seems so devoted to Iggy. And Reggie, well..." She paused, wrinkling her nose. "We both saw how he conducted himself at dinner that first night."

Elizabeth nodded, recalling Reggie's brazen behaviour – his shameless flirtation with Amelia and the tense exchange with Dominic Archer that followed. "You're right. It does seem implausible." Yet even as she spoke, a nagging voice reminded her that even the most unlikely scenarios sometimes held grains of truth.

"Speaking of men of questionable character," Meli said, her tone playful, "what about Mr Ashcroft? He seemed quite attentive last night."

Elizabeth felt warmth rising to her cheeks. "Oh, Meli, don't be absurd. Jonathan and I are merely … acquaintances."

"Acquaintances who dance rather closely," Meli teased. "And let's not forget Mr Bellini. His gaze hardly left you all evening. My goodness, Elizabeth, you seem to have them all falling at your feet."

The mention of Bellini sobered Elizabeth, her thoughts turning to Alfie, alone in his cell. Her smile faded as she considered the possibility of Bellini's involvement in Reggie's death.

Her gaze drifted to the rose garden. "I need to speak with Alfie again. Something about his account…" She paused, her brow creasing slightly. "I can't help feeling he's not being entirely honest with me. But first, I think we should return to the scene of the crime."

Meli's eyes widened. "The racecourse? You think the police might have missed something?"

Elizabeth considered for a moment. "We may notice something the police overlooked."

"When do we leave?" she asked, clasping her hands together.

"We? I hadn't–" Elizabeth began, but Meli quickly cut her off.

"Oh, please don't make me stay here, Elizabeth." Meli's shoulders slumped as she gazed imploringly at her cousin. "There's absolutely nothing to do here."

Elizabeth considered her cousin for a moment, then nodded. "Very well, you can come. But remember, we're there to investigate, not socialise."

Meli beamed, already gathering her bag and coat. "I'll be on my best behaviour, I promise."

The now familiar route to the racecourse slipped by, a blur of green fields and winding country lanes. On arrival, she parked behind a weathered, old shed, ensuring the Aston Martin wasn't visible from the racecourse.

"Right," she said, turning to Meli. "Remember why we're here."

Meli nodded, her expression serious. "To search for anything that might help Alfie."

"Exactly. And if anyone asks–"

"We're lost and looking for the ladies' room?"

"Perfect." Elizabeth smiled. "Shall we?"

Without waiting for an answer, she slipped out of the motorcar. Meli followed, closing her door with a soft click.

They crept towards the stables, their senses on high alert. As they drew closer, the pungent scent of hay, horses, and manure assaulted their senses. Just as they reached the stables, Elizabeth paused, catching the faint murmur of voices from one of the stalls.

Elizabeth's arm shot out, stopping Meli in her tracks. Pressing a finger to her lips, she gestured towards a nearby stack of hay bales. They ducked behind it, crouching low, and the rough straw scratched against their skin.

Elizabeth edged closer to her cousin. "Can you make out what they're saying?" she whispered.

Meli shook her head, straining to hear. The voices remained frustratingly indistinct, barely audible above the soft nickering of horses and the rustle of hay.

Elizabeth's gaze swept the stable yard, searching for cover. "We need to get closer," she whispered, already plotting their route.

Peering through a gap in the stall door, she caught sight of Dr Franklin hunched over a chestnut stallion, a syringe glinting in his hand. A stable hand hovered nearby, twisting his cap between nervous fingers.

"There we are," Franklin said, his tone low and satisfied as he withdrew the needle from the horse's neck. The stallion snorted softly, shaking its mane.

Franklin straightened, turning to the stable hand. "Take him to the paddock." He checked his watch. "Wait ten minutes, then put him through his paces. I want to see how he responds."

The stable hand nodded, reaching for the horse's bridle. "Yes, sir," he mumbled, leading the animal towards the door.

Elizabeth yanked Meli back, both flattening against the rough stable wall as the clip-clop of horse hooves approached. They held their breaths, watching a stable hand lead a chestnut past their hiding spot.

A shadow fell across the stable doorway as Antonio Bellini strode into view. His tailored suit looked absurdly out of place among the hay and horse tack.

Recognition flashed in Meli's eyes and she opened her mouth to call out to Antonio, but Elizabeth squeezed her arm, urging her to stay quiet.

"Franklin." The shout echoed off the stable walls.

Dr Franklin emerged from a nearby stall, wiping his hands on a rag. "Antonio … I wasn't expecting you."

Antonio's gaze swept the stable before settling on Franklin. "The boss is concerned about recent … developments. Black's death has brought unwanted scrutiny to our operations."

Franklin's fingers knotted in the rag, twisting it as he spoke. "Antonio … I assure you, I had no part in–"

Antonio cut him off with a flick of his hand. "The boss wants to ensure that his interests remain … protected." Antonio's tone remained level, but his eyes hardened. "You understand?"

Franklin swallowed hard as he nodded. "Of course. I'll keep my eyes open."

"See that you do," Antonio said. "Mr Bellini values loyalty above all else. If you notice anyone poking around or asking questions, you let me know. Capische?"

"You can count on me, Antonio," Franklin called, his words chasing Antonio's retreating back.

Alone, Franklin slumped against the stable wall, dabbing at his forehead with the grimy rag crumpled in his fist.

"Doc?" The stable hand reappeared. "The horse needs–"

Franklin's head turned, his eyes wild. "Not now!" he barked, sidestepping a feed bucket in his haste to get away.

The stable hand watched him go, then turned to a burly man mucking out a nearby stall. "Oi, Bucky, what's wrong with the doc?"

Elizabeth's ears pricked at the name. Bucky – Reggie's former trainer.

Bucky paused, leaning on his pitchfork as he stared after Franklin. "I'll have a word," he said, his gravelly voice low. He set the tool aside with a soft clang and followed Franklin's path.

They watched as Bucky swiped his grimy hands down the front of his work-worn trousers before pushing open the door without knocking. "Franklin? You in here?"

Elizabeth turned to Meli, her voice low. "I'll try to get closer and listen in. Keep watch, and if anyone comes–"

"I know," Meli replied with a playful flutter of her lashes. "I'll pretend I'm hopelessly lost and looking for the powder room."

She edged closer to the office, peering through the space between the frame and partially opened door.

Franklin's head snapped up as Bucky settled in one of the chairs, his fingers hastily working to roll down his shirt sleeve. "For God's sake, Bucky, haven't you heard of knocking?"

Elizabeth craned her neck for a better view, catching a glimpse of a small glass vial on Franklin's desk before his hand swept it out of sight.

"Couldn't help overhearing your chat with Bellini's boy," Bucky said, his tone gruff.

"Eavesdropping part of your job now, is it?" Franklin snarled, slipping his hand into his trouser pocket. "Reggie Black – even from the grave, he still manages to cause trouble."

Bucky lowered himself onto a nearby chair, his hand rubbing at his whiskery chin. "He always was a wrong 'un. Only looking out for himself."

"It's his fault I ended up in this mess. Black sold me out to Bellini to buy him some time on his gambling debts. I'm stuck under Bellini's thumb like the rest of them – with no way out." His hand dipped into his pocket, his shoulders tensing. "And now Bellini's not happy." He turned to face the window, his back to Bucky. "He thinks Reggie's death has brought too much attention ... and somehow it's all my fault."

A muscle twitched in Bucky's jaw as he watched Franklin, the weight of unspoken implications hanging between them.

"Don't get me wrong. I'd thought about doing it ... getting rid of him." Franklin paused, his hand hovering near the desk drawer. After a moment's hesitation, he pulled it open and retrieved a bottle of whisky. He held it up to

Bucky, who nodded. "But what purpose would it have served? The damage was already done."

"It might have made you feel better." Bucky grinned, revealing a row of stained, uneven teeth. "Might have made quite a few people feel better, I'd wager."

Franklin poured two measures into a pair of chipped mugs. He slid one across the desk to Bucky, spilling a few drops in the process. "Still, he got what he deserved in the end," Franklin said with a crooked half-smile.

Bucky grunted, his hand shaking slightly as lifted his mug. "To Reggie." He took a long swig, grimacing at the burn.

"To Reggie." Franklin finished, downing the rest of his whisky in one swift motion.

Bucky lifted his mug again, his gaze fixed on Franklin as he drained the last dregs. "You know, I've been thinking about Reggie's … accident." He set the empty mug down with a dull thud. "Word is that it wasn't the fall that killed him."

Franklin's fingers tightened around his own mug, a muscle twitching in his jaw. "Is that right?"

"Mm." Bucky nudged his empty mug across the desk. "Word is he died from an overdose of morphine."

Franklin's hand trembled slightly as he refilled Bucky's mug. "Careful, Bucky. That's dangerous talk."

"Is it?" Bucky's tone remained light, but his eyes never left Franklin's face. "I'm just saying … if someone had decided to take matters into their own hands … well, who would blame them?"

The room fell silent. Elizabeth held her breath, straining to hear more, but the two men simply stared at each other, the air between them thick with unspoken accusations.

Her mind worked quickly, piecing together the implications of what she'd just heard. Either one of these men could have been responsible for Reggie's death. Both men had unrestricted access to the stables, their presence there entirely ordinary. And Lord knows, each had motive enough to do it.

"Oh dear, I seem to have gotten lost looking for the powder room!" Meli's voice, pitched unnaturally high, pierced the air.

Elizabeth hurried over to where Meli stood with the stable hand. "There you are." She shook her head, fond exasperation in her voice. "You have the worst sense of direction. I distinctly told you to turn left, not right."

She slipped her hand through her cousin's arm. "Come on, I'll show you the way." With a swift turn, she steered them down the path, leaving the bewildered stable hand staring after them.

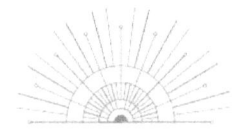

Chapter Eighteen

ELIZABETH GUNNED THE ENGINE, propelling the motorcar down the narrow lane away from Aintree. The racecourse vanished behind a bend, but the rush of their hasty departure still thrummed through her veins.

She exhaled slowly, her shoulders relaxing as she flicked a quick glance towards Meli before returning it to the road ahead. "That was far too close. If anyone besides that stable hand had spotted us…"

Meli's gaze darted to the rear-view mirror. "I half expect to see a posse of angry stable hands in pursuit on horseback. Though I hate that our investigation was cut short."

"Indeed," Elizabeth agreed, her mind already sifting through the information they'd collected.

"Still, I gathered enough to shed some light on our growing list of suspects."

Meli shifted in her seat, angling towards Elizabeth. Her fingers drummed a quick, impatient rhythm on the leather upholstery. "Well? Don't keep me in suspense."

Elizabeth relayed what she'd overheard. "It seems Reggie shared some secret he'd uncovered about Dr Franklin with Mr Bellini. Now Bellini's using it to blackmail him."

"Good heavens." Meli gasped, her eyes widening. "No wonder the doctor behaved the way he did around Reggie that day at Rosewood Park."

"Indeed." Elizabeth nodded, recalling their first meeting with Dr Franklin at the stables. There had been something off about his behaviour towards Reggie, something more than just mere animosity. His excessive sweating and nervous energy took on new meaning now. The image of the glass vial on his desk at the track resurfaced in her mind. She paused, piecing it all together before voicing her suspicions. "Meli … I think Dr Franklin might be addicted to opiates."

Meli's breath caught. "Are you certain?"

Elizabeth's hands tightened on the steering wheel. "As certain as I can be without catching him in the act. Remember when I found him in his car at Rosewood Park? He seemed ... absent, almost disconnected from reality. And those small blood spots on his shirt sleeve – I suspect he'd just administered a dose."

"What about Reggie's comment on the doctor's morning fix? I thought he meant coffee, but ... Could this be what Mr Bellini is using against him?"

"If Bellini knows about Franklin's addiction, it would be powerful leverage indeed."

"So the doctor had a motive to want rid of Reggie."

"A compelling one, at that." Elizabeth's gaze flicked between the road and the rear-view mirror. "An addiction like that could ruin his career and reputation in an instant."

"What about Bucky? You mentioned he'd staked his career on Reggie."

"Not just his career. When Reggie left, Bucky lost everything." Elizabeth's grip tightened on the steering wheel. "That kind of betrayal could push someone to extremes. He'd spent years grooming Reggie for success, only for him to dump Bucky when he made it."

A shadow of sadness crossed Meli's face. "It's hard to say which is worse – the fear of losing everything or the pain of having already lost it."

"And desperation, whether from fear or loss, can drive people to dangerous extremes."

Meli's gaze darted between Elizabeth and the road ahead. "What about the others? Do we have any other credible suspects?"

Elizabeth tapped her fingers on the steering wheel. "Dominic Archer springs to mind. He claims to be in love with Miss Stanford, and her dalliance with Reggie must have stung."

"He did lose his temper that night at dinner," Meli reminded Elizabeth. "But surely that's not enough to–"

"Perhaps not on its own," Elizabeth interjected. "But coupled with Mr Archer's questionable past and apparently opportunistic nature, it paints a concerning picture."

Meli hesitated as if pondering her words. "And Miss Stanford herself? Could she perhaps … have committed the unthinkable?"

Elizabeth's eyes narrowed as she considered the possibility. "Her affection for Reggie seemed genuine. But if the gossip about his reputation with women holds any truth, well ... hell hath no fury, as they say."

"True ... but still, I can't quite believe it of Miss Stanford," Meli said, a crease forming between her brows. "Now Mr Bellini, on the other hand ... Do you think he could be involved in Reggie's murder?"

Elizabeth considered this for a moment. "It's possible, but it doesn't quite add up. Reggie might have been a liability, but his death has brought unwanted scrutiny to the racecourse and, by extension, Bellini's business interests." She frowned, piecing together the puzzle. "Reggie likely sold out numerous people to Bellini to save his own skin, not just Franklin. That information would be invaluable to a man like Bellini – leverage he could likely use to further his operations."

"Miss Stanford's comment about Georgia and Reggie ... I can't stop thinking about it."

Elizabeth's eyes darted briefly to her cousin before returning to the road. "What about it?"

Meli opened her mouth, then closed it again. She tried again, the words tumbling out in a rush. "If what she said was true... Do you think Iggy could have played a role in Reggie's death?"

The question hung in the air, heavy and uncomfortable. Elizabeth exhaled slowly as she pondered the Fairfaxes' marriage.

Before Iggy's accident, they were globe-trotting adventurers, perfectly matched in their zest for life. Now, their world had shrunk to Rosewood Park's boundaries. Gone were the shared thrills of exploration, and the difference in their ages and desires seemed more pronounced than ever.

She recalled snippets of heated exchanges behind closed doors. Georgia's insistence on going into business with Enzo Bellini, despite Iggy's clear disapproval, had fuelled more than one heated conversation.

Then there were Georgia's solo visits to Adelina's.

"I don't know, Meli." Elizabeth eased off the accelerator as they approached a bend in the road.

"Their marriage has certainly been under strain. But murder? That's quite a leap."

They drove the rest of the way in silence, each lost in thought, the weight of Elizabeth's words settling between them.

She brought the motorcar to a halt before the Aintree police station.

Meli eyed the gloomy building as she reached for the door. "It's every bit as bleak as I imagined."

Elizabeth caught Meli's gaze in the rear-view mirror. "It's probably prudent if you wait here. You know how the Chief Inspector feels about Alfie … and women, for that matter."

Meli crossed her arms, her lips pressing into a thin line. She glanced at the station, then back at Elizabeth. "You're probably right."

Elizabeth gripped the door handle, her eyes drifting to Thornton's Pawnbrokers down the street. "Meli, you will stay in the car, won't you?"

"I thought I might take a stroll along the high street, perhaps browse in some of the shops."

Elizabeth frowned. She couldn't risk Meli wandering into Thorntons and getting entangled in whatever Sam Thornton was involved in. "I'd prefer it if you stayed here."

"Do I have to?" Meli let out a long sigh, her shoulders slumping.

"Yes," Elizabeth insisted, her tone brooking no argument. She understood her young cousin's desire to explore, but Meli's insatiable curiosity was also a constant source of worry. "I won't be long."

She stepped out of the motorcar. Squaring her shoulders, she climbed the front steps, her mind focused on the task ahead.

The usual cacophony of sounds assaulted her ears the moment she entered the police station. She paused, taking a deep breath before making her way towards the front desk. A young constable glanced up from his paperwork, his pen hovering mid-sentence as he took her in.

"Can I help you, miss?" The constable set his pen down as he got to his feet.

Elizabeth offered a polite smile. "I'd like to speak with Alfie Tanner on a matter of great importance."

"I'm afraid that's not possible, miss. The Chief Inspector's out and left strict instructions that no one was to see the lad while he was gone. If I let you see him, miss, he'll have my guts for garters."

Elizabeth tilted her head slightly, her hazel eyes meeting the constable's gaze. As she spoke, her hand brushed lightly against his arm. "I appreciate your dilemma. However, Mr Tanner may have information crucial to the Reggie Black case. Surely the Chief Inspector would want us to pursue every lead?"

The constable shifted his weight, his eyes darting between Elizabeth and the shadowy hallway. "Five minutes, miss," he muttered, tapping the face of his pocket watch. "And I'll be counting every second."

Elizabeth waited as he rounded his desk, his keys clinking softly. She followed, descending a narrow staircase, the air cooling with each step. The stench of damp stone and unwashed bodies assaulted her nostrils. At the bottom, she squinted in the dim light cast by a single bulb, which barely illuminated the row of iron-barred cells.

Alfie glanced up as Elizabeth neared the cell. Shadows lurked beneath his eyes, his usually weather-beaten face now as pale as chalk. He eased himself into a sitting position, wincing at the effort. "Lady Elizabeth?" A weak smile tugged at his lips. "Didn't expect to see you back so soon."

Her heart clenched at the sight of him. Crafting a steady smile, she asked, "How are you holding up?"

His lips twitched in a ghost of his usual grin. "Can't complain," he said, voice brittle. "Any news?"

Elizabeth inched closer. "We're making progress. Lord Hawthorne's engaged a top barrister, should the matter go before the courts."

Alfie's throat bobbed as he swallowed. "What's to become of me … if they find me guilty?"

"We must stay positive," she insisted, trying to avoid voicing the inevitable. "We're doing our best to get to the bottom of this, but I can't help feeling you're holding something back … that you haven't been entirely truthful with me."

"I didn't push him, Lady Elizabeth, I swear … I might have swiped his arm away, to stop him from pushing me, but I didn't unseat him." The words tumbled out in a jumble.

"I believe you … we all do. But that's not what I meant."

Alfie frowned.

"I'm talking about the night Mr Thornton was attacked."

"I don't understand." The creases on his forehead deepened, his eyes darting around the poorly lit space. "What's that got to do with Reggie's death?"

"I don't have much time. The constable will be back any minute. I'm trying my best to help you, but unless you tell me everything, then…" She stopped herself short, unable to put his fate into words. "I believe the reason the Chief Inspector is so intent on pinning this murder on you is because he thinks you are responsible for the attack on Mr Thornton. He sees this as a way of writing a wrong, so to speak."

His fingers twisted in his lap, his eyes downcast.

"I know you didn't attack Mr Thornton … but I think you know who did."

The silence stretched.

"Revealing the true attacker to the Chief Inspector might compel him to set aside his prejudice and seek Mr Black's actual murderer."

The longer the silence stretched, the more she realised his fear.

"I … I can't." Alfie's voice faltered, the words catching in his throat.

Elizabeth hesitated, her stomach twisting. "Alfie, listen to me." Her voice dropped to a whisper. "If you don't tell me what happened, you could be…" She swallowed hard. "You have to tell me."

The young jockey jerked upright, eyes bulging. "The gallows?" His whisper rasped, cheeks blanching. "But I didn't–"

"I need you to trust me, Alfie." Elizabeth leaned in, her gaze locking with his. "Whatever you saw, whatever you know, it could clear your name. But I can't help unless you tell me."

Alfie's eyes flitted from corner to corner, his shoulders hunched. He exhaled sharply.

Alfie hunched forward, lowering his voice. "Sam Thornton and his father were at each other's throats," he said. "Mr Thornton was shouting that Sam had been fiddling the books and something about Bellini's dirty money. Said it had to stop."

Alfie's hands trembled. "Then Sam … he grabbed something. Swung it at his father's head when he turned his back."

He swallowed hard. "There was so much blood. I tried to run, but Sam caught me. Threatened to tell Bellini if I squealed." His voice cracked. "And everyone knows what Bellini does to grasses."

Enzo Bellini. Elizabeth's mind reeled. Why did all roads ultimately lead back to him?

His criminal web spread further than she had ever imagined. No wonder Alfie had been so afraid to speak up.

And Sam Thornton … Elizabeth's fingers curled into fists. What sort of man would attack his own father, then frame an innocent lad, all for the sake of a few ill-gotten pounds?

"Time's up, miss," the constable called.

Elizabeth's thoughts swirled. Revealing Sam Thornton as the attacker would expose Enzo's connection, potentially endangering Alfie.

She needed a plan, and fast.

"Alfie, not a word of this to anyone, understood?"

"Even the Chief Inspector?"

"Him least of all." Her tone softened. "Trust me, I'll sort this out. Can you stay strong a bit longer?"

Alfie's chin dipped in a weak nod.

"Miss, I must insist," the constable pressed.

Elizabeth's hand lingered on the bars. Leaving Alfie felt wrong, but for now, these cold bars offered him more protection than she could.

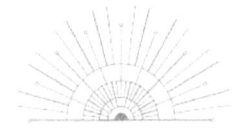

Chapter Nineteen

ELIZABETH EXITED THE POLICE station, Alfie's confession churning in her thoughts. She approached the Aston Martin, where Meli was waiting, her face the picture of boredom.

As Elizabeth slid into the driver's seat, Meli perked up. "About time! I was beginning to think you'd moved in. How is Alfie holding up?"

"He's putting on a brave face, but I could see the strain in his eyes. The poor boy looks like he hasn't slept in days."

"Did you learn anything new?" Meli's eyes searched Elizabeth's face as the Aston Martin's engine purred to life. Elizabeth nodded as she guided the motorcar into the traffic street.

Meli listened intently as Elizabeth recounted Alfie's revelation, her expression shifting from surprise to concern. When Elizabeth finished, Meli shook her head in disbelief. "Poor Alfie. No wonder he's been so frightened."

"Indeed." Elizabeth's jaw tightened as she navigated through the traffic. "It seems Mr Bellini's business interests are wide and varied, and most of them are illegal."

Meli's hand flew to her mouth, eyes wide with shock. "Good heavens! And poor Alfie, trapped in the middle, too afraid of Bellini's wrath to speak up."

Nodding grimly, Elizabeth met Meli's eyes in the rear-view mirror. "Which is why I'll need the help of Mr Ashcroft."

"Ah, the dashing Mr Ashcroft. And where do you plan on finding him?"

"Adelina's."

Sitting up straighter, Meli's expression brightened. "Splendid idea. Perhaps I'll get to have a flutter in Adelina's illicit gambling den."

When Elizabeth opened her mouth to protest, Meli raised a hand. "Relax, I'm just joking. Well, about the gambling, but I insist on coming with you. I can be your lookout, or perhaps distract Antonio, if he's there."

"Fine," Elizabeth said, her fingers drumming on the steering wheel. "But promise me you'll be careful. Enzo Bellini is as dangerous as he is charming."

Meli twisted in her seat to face Elizabeth. "Do you think we should invite Georgia to join us?"

Elizabeth's brow furrowed as she navigated a turn. "Probably best not to. Iggy wasn't very happy the last time she went to Adelina's. We don't want to cause any more tension between them."

"You're right." Meli slumped back. "The last thing we want is to complicate matters further."

Hedgerows whizzed by as Elizabeth navigated the winding country lane. Rounding a bend, she caught sight of Georgia's ivory Vauxhall at the roadside.

Elizabeth eased off the accelerator. "Speak of the devil."

As they drew to a stop alongside the Vauxhall, Georgia's head popped up from behind the motorcar.

Elizabeth leaned out the window. "Georgia, what on earth? Is everything alright?"

Georgia straightened, wiping her greasy hands on a rag. "Nothing major, just a little puncture."

"Hop in, we're on our way back to Rosewood Park." Elizabeth gestured towards the back seat. "We can arrange for someone to come back and fix it."

Georgia waved a dismissive hand. "No need, honey. It's all fixed."

Meli leaned forward, her eyes wide. "You changed it yourself?"

"Easy as pie, honey." Georgia bent to secure the clips on the spare wheel cover. A flash of gold and teal silk caught Elizabeth's eye. She watched as Georgia hastily stuffed it back inside the cover.

Elizabeth's thoughts churned. The silk was unmistakeable – Alfie's racing colours

But what on earth was it doing hidden in the cover of Georgia's wheel cover?

Georgia dusted off her hands. "Well, I'd best be on my way."

"Back to Rosewood Park?"

"Not just yet. I need to pick up some veterinary supplies from Dr Franklin."

"I hope one of the horses isn't ill?" Meli asked.

"Oh, nothing to worry about, honey. Just routine supplies." Georgia's smile didn't quite reach her eyes as she climbed into her Vauxhall. "I'll catch up with you both later at Rosewood." The motorcar's engine roared, and she sped off, leaving a cloud of dust in her wake.

Elizabeth watched Georgia's Vauxhall disappear around the bend, her thoughts racing. She eased the Aston Martin back onto the road.

"Did you see that cloth in Georgia's wheel cover?"

"What of it?" Meli shrugged. "Probably just a scrap of leftover material she's using as a rag."

"It looked exactly like Alfie's riding colours, Meli."

"It could've been anything. A flag or bunting perhaps?" Meli's gaze flicked between Elizabeth and the passing countryside. "You know how Georgia adores teal and gold."

Meli was probably right. She shook her head, trying to clear her thoughts. Perhaps she was reading too much into things. Since her visit to Alfie, she'd been all at sixes and sevens. Or was it the thought of seeing Jonathan Ashcroft again that was the cause of her unease?"

The Aston Martin hugged the winding road, Rosewood Park's facade emerging in the distance.

Meli sighed as they drew nearer. "I must confess, Elizabeth, I shan't be sorry to return to London and be far away from this dreary, old place."

Elizabeth guided the Aston Martin into the garage at Rosewood Park, the engine's purr fading as she cut the ignition. She stepped out, her gaze sweeping over the house. Its windows were dark, the facade silent in the fading light.

Meli followed, pulling her coat tighter as they crossed the gravel path.

The warmth enveloped them the moment they entered the house, chasing away the evening's chill. Elizabeth paused, her head cocked. The usual bustle of the household was absent.

Pritchard appeared from the drawing room, his customary poise slightly off-kilter.

"Good evening, Pritchard." Elizabeth's gaze swept the empty spaces. "It's very quiet this evening. Isn't Lord Fairfax at home?"

"He's in his room, my lady. A little out of sorts today," he replied, concern flitting across his face.

Elizabeth's shoulders relaxed. Iggy might be young at heart, but that motorcar crash had left its mark. Who knew what lingering effects it might have had? "Please give him my best wishes for a speedy recovery, Pritchard."

"Certainly, my lady."

"Oh, and, Pritchard? Please inform Mrs Langley that Miss Diomaros and I won't be home for dinner this evening."

"Certainly, my lady."

As they climbed the stairs, Elizabeth's thoughts raced ahead to Adelina's. Would Jonathan Ashcroft be there? She had no way of knowing, but the alternative – asking Mr Bellini for Jonathan's address – risked tipping her hand.

But she didn't have time to dwell on whether Jonathan would be there or not. She'd cross that bridge if, and when, she came to it.

Scanning the contents of the wardrobe, she selected a Madeleine Vionnet gown in a shade of plum. The silk rippled in her hands, its deep hue complemented by intricate silver beadwork along the neckline and hem.

Across the room, Meli held up a sapphire gown, its beaded fringe shimmering in the electric light.

While Elizabeth secured a marquisate comb in her inky-dark tresses, Meli wrestled her dark curls into a faux bob.

Finally satisfied with the end result, Meli slipped on a pair of silver T-strap shoes before draping a gossamer shawl over her shoulders.

With a final swipe of lipstick, Elizabeth met her cousin's eyes in the mirror. "Shall we?"

Meli nodded, grabbing her silver clutch.

After giving their appearances a final glance in the mirror, they made their way through the empty house, the silence almost as oppressive as the gloom. "I can't even begin to imagine how cheerless this house must feel in the dead of winter." Meli shuddered, slipping her hand through Elizabeth's arm. "I'm sure it would feel rather eerie."

"You and your imagination," Elizabeth said with a chuckle as they stepped into the cool night air and made their way to the garage.

She slipped into the driver's seat and started up the engine, her mind already racing with the implications of what might await them at Adelina's.

The countryside faded into Liverpool's urban sprawl. Elizabeth guided the motorcar through narrow streets until they reached their destination.

They stepped out onto the cobblestones before Adelina's unassuming entrance. Inside, the seductive notes of a saxophone mingled with the low murmur of conversation and laughter. Cigarette smoke hung in lazy coils, briefly illuminated by the electric sconces adorning the mahogany walls. The hostess approached, her sequined dress shimmering like liquid mercury.

"Good evening, ladies." The hostess's crimson lips curved into a practised smile. "Table for two?"

Elizabeth's gaze darted from the bustling bar to the shadowy corners, then settled on the empty VIP table. "Yes, just the two of us tonight."

The hostess steered them past the coveted VIP section and instead settled them at a secluded booth tucked away in a corner.

"Will Mr Bellini be in this evening?"

"Who knows with Mr Bellini?" She shrugged, a smug smile playing on her lips. "But you're welcome to hang around, see if he may make an appearance later."

Elizabeth's spine stiffened, her eyes meeting the hostess's with glacial composure. The slight was meant to rattle her, to lump her in with Bellini's fluttering entourage. But Elizabeth wouldn't give this woman the pleasure of seeing her squirm.

"Two gin fizzes, please," she said, her words crisp and pointed as icicles.

"Of course." The hostess's smile tightened, her eyes flicking away. "I'll have a waiter bring your order." She pivoted sharply, sequins flashing as she retreated into the crowd.

"It seems Mr Bellini is quite popular among the ladies."

Elizabeth's eyebrow arched. "So it would seem." Her fingers drummed lightly on the table as her gaze swept across the club, lingering on each shadowy alcove and crowded table.

Meli leaned in, her whisper barely audible. "Can you see him?"

Elizabeth shook her head. Her attention drifted to the far corner where the velvet curtain hung. A silver-haired gentleman paused before it, adjusted his waistcoat, and slipped behind the folds.

Another patron approached the curtain, younger this time. He glanced over his shoulder before vanishing from view.

Elizabeth turned to Meli. "Will you be alright here if I visit Adelina's other VIP area?"

"Can't I come with you?"

"I only have one pin." Elizabeth retrieved the silver pin from her clutch.

Meli's eyes lit up. "Couldn't I just say I've lost mine?"

"We can't risk drawing attention. I'll slip in quickly to check for Mr Ashcroft."

"But what if you run into Miss Stanford? Or someone else?"

"Then I'll just have to ensure I don't."

Meli bit her lip, worry creasing her brow. "It sounds awfully risky. Are you sure there isn't another way to locate Mr Ashcroft?"

"I've told you, Meli. The man's practically a ghost. Just pops up when you least expect it. And I can't exactly ask Bellini for an address, can I?"

"I suppose not." Meli's shoulders drooped.

The waiter materialised and placed two gin fizzes before them with practiced precision. He vanished as swiftly as he'd appeared, leaving behind only the faint scent of juniper and lime.

Elizabeth rose, then quickly sat back down.

"What is it?" Meli asked.

"Antonio." Elizabeth nodded towards the velvet curtain where Antonio stood.

"I'll distract him while you … do what you need to do." Meli stood. "But be careful."

"You too," Elizabeth replied.

She watched over the rim of her glass as Meli approached Antonio. Her cousin's charm worked its magic, and within moments, they were weaving through the crowd towards the dance floor, Antonio's attention fully captured.

Elizabeth set her drink aside and sauntered towards the artwork flanking the curtain. Her fingers, steady despite the risk, affixed the silver pin to her dress. She cast a final, sweeping glance across the room before easing into the shadowy alcove.

She slipped behind the curtain, drawing a steadying breath. She raised her hand and knocked: two quick, a pause, three more. The hatch slid open. Dark eyes met hers, then dropped to the silver pin on her dress and the door groaned open.

Elizabeth stepped into the gambling den, her posture relaxed but her senses alert. The familiar haze of cigar smoke and the clink of chips greeted her. She scanned the room, noting the positions of the tables and the patrons hunched over their games.

The hostess from her previous visit caught her eye and offered a subtle nod of recognition. Elizabeth returned the gesture, grateful for the discretion.

Her gaze swept the room, searching for Amelia or Jonathan. Finding neither, she continued her survey.

A flash of movement caught her eye. The young man she'd seen speaking with Enzo during her last visit eased through a door in the wall – the same one Enzo had used before. He held it ajar, engaged in conversation with a blond man dressed in a similar style.

She edged closer, plucking a flute of champagne from a passing waiter's tray. As she positioned herself within earshot, her hand drifted to a nearby table, fingers stealthily palming a high-value chip.

"…just heard from the boss," the darker-haired man said. "He'll be here later tonight."

With Bellini's absence confirmed, Elizabeth seized her chance. She swayed slightly, her movements exaggerated as she affected a tipsy demeanour. With a calculated misstep, she bumped into the blond man. Her champagne sloshed over the rim, golden droplets spattering his pristine white shirt.

"Oh, I'm terribly sorry!" she slurred, pawing at the stain. Her gaze flicked past the man, catching a glimpse of a well-lit, empty office beyond the door. As she steadied herself against the frame, her fingers deftly wedged the chip into the gap.

"Go change that shirt," the darker-haired man ordered his colleague. To Elizabeth, he added smoothly, "No harm done, miss. Why don't you have a seat until you're steadier on your feet?"

"I think I've had a little too much champagne," she said, swaying slightly.

Elizabeth watched the darker-haired man vanish through the main door. A quick glance confirmed that the chip, barely visible, had done its job, holding the door just wide enough for her to slip her fingers into the gap. With a final glance around the room, she eased it open before disappearing through it.

Elizabeth shut the door behind her, the brightness of the office catching her off guard. She scanned the room, her eyes adjusting to the stark light that left her feeling exposed.

She eased open desk drawers, not quite sure what she was looking for. Financial records, incriminating evidence – anything could be crucial.

A leather-bound notebook drew her attention. She opened it, her brow furrowing at the

Italian script. The figures, however, spoke volumes. Column after column of numbers, far too large for any legitimate business. This could be it.

Footsteps echoed in the corridor outside.

Her gaze swept the room for any means of escape. None.

Had Bellini returned early?

Her mind raced through potential explanations, each less plausible than the last.

The footsteps drew nearer.

A nearby clock ticked, counting down the seconds.

Her breath hitched as the handle turned…

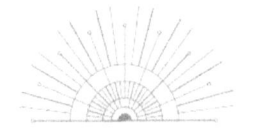

Chapter Twenty

THE HANDLE RATTLED AS the door eased open. Her gaze flicked to the window – too high, too small for escape. She braced herself for the worst.

Jonathan Ashcroft stood in the doorway, his green eyes widening as they locked with hers.

Her breath caught. "Jonathan?"

He slipped inside and eased the door shut. "What in God's name are you doing here?" he hissed, scanning the room.

Elizabeth opened her mouth to speak, but Jonathan shook his head, cutting her off. "On second thoughts, let's come back to that. I need to get you out of here. Now."

"Excuse me? What makes you so sure I can't get myself out of here?"

"Can you?"

"Well … I haven't had a chance to assess the situation yet."

"As much I'd be happy to stand around discussing your many skills, now is not the time … if Enzo or one of his henchmen find you … or me for that matter, in here … trust me, they won't bother asking why."

Jonathan jerked his head towards the door he'd entered through. "Come on, this way."

"I'm not leaving without Meli. She's in the main club."

His jaw tightened, a muscle flickering beneath his skin as he turned back to the gambling den door. His fingers traced the woodwork, finding a concealed panel. With a soft click, it slid open to reveal a hidden spyhole.

He peered through the spyhole, his shoulders stiffening. "Damn."

"What is it?"

"One of Bellini's henchmen is guarding the door."

"What about the other door? Can't we get out that way?"

"Too risky." He shook his head. "We'd be walking right into Bellini's territory without knowing who or what might be waiting for us."

Elizabeth moved towards the desk and grabbed the leather-bound notebook.

"What are you doing?" Jonathan's voice was sharp.

"It's evidence," Elizabeth said, her grip tightening on the notebook. "I'm sure the police will find it very useful."

"Leave it. Once Bellini notices it's missing, he'll destroy everything that links him to any illegal operations."

Elizabeth's fingers tightened on the notebook. If it contained information linking Bellini to Sam Thornton, it could corroborate Alfie's story and clear his name. Yet removing it might alert Bellini, potentially derailing a larger investigation into his criminal empire. Elizabeth hesitated, weighing the immediate benefit against the broader consequences.

"Elizabeth." Jonathan's voice dropped.

With a frustrated sigh, she placed the notebook back inside the drawer, a gleam of gunmetal catching her eye. She glanced at Jonathan.

Before either could speak, voices drifted in from the corridor, followed by the unmistakable sound of approaching footsteps.

Jonathan grabbed her hand. "This way," he murmured, pulling her towards what appeared to be a solid wall. With a gentle push, a hidden panel swung open, revealing another, slightly bigger room barely illuminated by dimly lit wall sconces. A large, circular table covered in green baize dominated the centre, surrounded by plush leather chairs. In one corner, a small but well-stocked bar gleamed with crystal decanters and polished glasses.

"Secret rooms, hidden doors – nothing's as it seems with Bellini, is it? It's all smoke and mirrors."

"I told you, Enzo Bellini is a dangerous man," Jonathan said. "He doesn't take chances. This whole place is like a labyrinth, filled with secret rooms and escape routes."

"A private gambling den for Bellini's inner circle, I presume?" she asked, eyeing the table.

"You could say that … it's where Bellini entertains his … like-minded business associates, shall we say."

"How do you know so much about Bellini and his business?"

"Ssh!" Jonathan pressed a finger to his lips at the sound of the office door opening. They ducked behind the bar, crouching low as voices grew louder and footsteps approached.

A chill crept across Elizabeth's skin as she recognised Enzo Bellini's voice drifting through the walls. They were trapped, mere inches away from discovery, with only a thin barrier separating them.

"I overheard Bellini's men say he wouldn't be in until later," she whispered, her words barely disturbing the air between them.

Jonathan's lips quirked in a humourless smile. "That's Bellini's way. He cultivates uncertainty. Keeps his people guessing, always on edge."

"The police have been sniffing around the track," a gruff voice said. "Asking questions about Reggie's death."

"Did they find anything?" Bellini's tone was sharp.

"I don't think so."

"Did you move everything like I told you?"

"Yeah, moved it all to her ladyship's place."

Elizabeth's mind raced. They must be talking about Georgia. Was this why Enzo had been so keen to go into business with her? To use her stables as a front for one of his operations? Georgia wasn't stupid, far from it. Surely she must know about Enzo and his shady practices. No wonder Iggy was so against it. But the question remained: why had Georgia agreed to it?

"Franklin's becoming a liability," the other man continued. "He's so dosed most of the time, he can't tell which end of the needle to use."

"Get Antonio to keep an eye on him," Bellini said, his voice low. "Reggie's death was … unfortunate," Bellini said. "Still, he had his uses. His knack for losing at cards and the debts he accumulated made him quite … pliable. Willing to sell out anyone to save his own skin."

There was a brief pause before Bellini continued, "Without Reggie's loose lips, we'd never have learned about Franklin's habit. Or her ladyship's … little secret."

Elizabeth's breath caught in her throat as she processed Bellini's words. What secret could Georgia be harbouring? It must be something truly serious for Bellini to wield such leverage over her.

Unbidden, Amelia's snide remark came to mind. "I don't know what Reggie saw in her." Could Georgia and Reggie have been having an affair?

Elizabeth's stomach twisted at the thought, but even as the possibility formed, she dismissed it. No, an affair wouldn't be enough to force Georgia into business with a man like Enzo Bellini. There had to be more to it, something far more serious.

"Make some enquiries," Bellini continued. "See if there's anyone else with a mouth as big as Reggie's."

"There's Sam Thornton. Word is, he's in deep with Snowy Fitzgibbon."

"Thornton?" Bellini mused. "Why does that name sound familiar?"

"We use his old man's shop to clean some of the track money. And that fake antique business of his has been useful for our import ventures."

"Ah, yes," Bellini said. "Keep a close eye on young Thornton. We might need to … adjust our arrangement."

Elizabeth's muscles tensed at Bellini's words, acutely aware of how precarious their position was.

Without warning, Bellini's office door flew open.

"Boss, Darby Sabini's just arrived, with a couple of his men. He's in the club."

Bellini's voice cut through the air, sharp as a razor. "Sabini? Here?" A heavy silence fell, broken only by the slow scrape of a chair against the floor. When Bellini spoke again, his tone was cold and deliberate. "Round up every man we've got. I want them in the club, now. Make sure Sabini sees exactly who he's dealing with while I … entertain our unexpected guest."

She held her breath as Bellini's voice faded, followed by the shuffle of multiple feet. The door clicked shut. She met Jonathan's eyes in the dim light, straining to hear any lingering presence in the office. Seconds stretched like hours until, finally, silence settled over them.

Jonathan's voice was barely a whisper. "Now's our chance."

He eased the secret panel open and his gaze swept the empty office beyond. He nodded to Elizabeth and slipped out, then she followed close behind. At the door to the gambling den, Jonathan paused, eye pressed to the spyhole.

"Clear," he murmured. "Act natural but try not to make eye contact with anyone."

They stepped into the den. The din of voices and glasses enveloped them. Elizabeth scanned the crowd, her heart sinking as she failed to spot Meli.

Inside, the gambling den was business as usual, the air thick with cigar smoke and the clatter of chips. Elizabeth noted only a handful of Bellini's men remained, stationed near the entrance. The rest, she surmised, had been called away to deal with the unexpected arrival of Sabini.

Jonathan's gaze swept the room, pausing briefly on a nearby roulette table. "Slow down. We don't want to draw attention."

Elizabeth's eyes darted towards the exit. "I need to get back to Meli, especially with this Sabini character out there."

"You know who he is?"

"No, but I doubt he's a choir boy if he's got Bellini so spooked."

Jonathan's jaw tightened. "Darby Sabini's got a stranglehold on racecourse gambling in the south. He's been pushing into Manchester and Liverpool, trying to expand his territory northwards.

"Why do you suppose he's here?"

Jonathan scanned the room before speaking. "Sabini showing up here tonight … it's no accident."

Elizabeth glanced at him, her steps slowing. "What's he after?"

"Sizing up the competition," Jonathan murmured, his voice low as they passed a table. "Bellini's got control here, but Sabini's been watching. Coming into his club – it's Sabini's way of testing the waters. Checking if Bellini's really as strong as his reputation suggests."

Elizabeth cast a quick look around. "And if he's not?"

"Then Sabini will make his move," Jonathan said, his eyes flicking to a corner table. "He's not here for a friendly visit. If Bellini stumbles, Sabini will be all over him. This is more than a meeting – it's a power play."

"You don't think there'll be trouble, do you?"

"Not here. Too public." Jonathan's eyes darted towards the exit. "But I'd rather not take chances. We need to find Meli and get you both out of here."

Elizabeth nodded, swallowing her instinct to argue that she could take care of herself. Meli's safety trumped her pride.

Bellini's henchman eyed them warily before stepping aside to grant them access back into the main club. As soon as they'd cleared the velvet curtain, her eyes swept the crowded room, landing on their original table. A group of strangers now occupied it, laughing over cocktails.

She and Jonathan wove through the crowds, heads bowed to avoid catching Enzo's eye. The clink of glasses and the hum of conversation masked their approach to the hostess stand.

Elizabeth leaned in, keeping her voice low. "Excuse me, have you seen my cousin? The young woman I was with earlier?"

The hostess's gaze lingered on Jonathan, her painted lips curving into a knowing smile. Elizabeth bristled, recalling the woman's earlier insinuations about Bellini.

"Oh, you mean the dark-haired girl? She left a while ago."

Elizabeth's gaze swept the club once more, her stomach knotting. No sign of Antonio. She didn't know if this was a good sign or not. "Did you happen to notice if she left with anyone?"

"Sorry," she said, examining her crimson nails. "I've been a little busy."

Elizabeth turned to Jonathan, her voice low and urgent. "We have to find her."

They raced out of the club into the cool night air. Elizabeth's thoughts tumbled as they hurried back to Iggy's motorcar. Rounding the corner, she spotted Meli leaning against the bonnet.

"Meli!" Elizabeth called. "What on earth are you doing out here? Why did you leave the club?"

Meli rolled her eyes. "That Antonio is all muscle and no mind. I had to make up an excuse about leaving just to get away from him."

Elizabeth rushed to Meli, her hands trembling as she grasped her cousin's arms.

"Sorry." Meli's tone was far from contrite. "But honestly, he's such a bore. All he does is talk about himself." Her gaze flicked to Jonathan, a mischievous glint in her eye. "I see you found who you were looking for."

Jonathan's eyebrows shot up, his gaze darting between Meli and Elizabeth.

Elizabeth turned to Meli. "I'll fill you in on the way home." She shifted her attention to Jonathan. "Can we drop you off somewhere, Mr Ashcroft?"

"Thank you, but no. I think I'll head back to Adelina's. Fancy a nightcap and perhaps a turn at the tables."

Elizabeth locked eyes with Jonathan. Understanding flashed between them. He intended to return and keep watch over Bellini and Sabini.

She swallowed hard. "Be careful."

"Caution is my watchword, Lady Elizabeth." Jonathan swept into a slight bow, his charm on full display. "Now if you'll excuse me, I bid you both a pleasant evening."

She watched him leave, dread coiling in the pit of her stomach. Jonathan was walking back into the viper's nest, and she was powerless to stop him.

She turned to Meli. "Come on, let's head home. I've so much to tell you."

Chapter Twenty-One

ELIZABETH FLOORED THE ACCELERATOR, the Aston Martin surging forward as if sharing her urgency to escape Adelina's web of secrets. Her pulse quickened, not from the speed, but from the gravity of their discoveries.

Meli's eyes widened as Elizabeth recounted everything she'd learned at Adelina's. When she finished, Meli let out a low whistle. "I can't believe how deep this goes," she said, shaking her head. "Bellini, Dr Franklin, even Georgia … it's like a giant spider's web, and poor Alfie's caught right in the middle."

"Indeed." Her fingers flexed, then tightened on the steering wheel. "And we need to untangle it before he pays the price for someone else's misdeeds."

She guided the Aston Martin into Rosewood Park's garage and cut the engine. As the purr of the motor faded, Meli turned to her, a crease forming between her brows.

"What do you think Bellini was referring to when he mentioned moving something here."

Elizabeth exhaled slowly, allowing herself a moment to gather her thoughts. "Dirty money, opiates, who knows?"

"Opiates?" Meli's voice pitched higher. "You think Bellini is peddling opiates?"

"It's possible. We already know he's involved in a number of other illegal activities, so it wouldn't surprise me in the slightest if he was involved in the drug trade as well."

"Where do you think he'd hide them?" Meli asked.

Elizabeth paused, her mind working through the possibilities. "The stables. There's constant activity, and no one would question extra supplies or packages being moved in and out. Not to mention plenty of places to hide things."

"I still don't understand why Georgia would allow him to do this. Do you think she had an affair with Mr Black and Bellini found out?"

Elizabeth frowned. "I don't think so. Whatever Bellini's holding over her, it must be far more serious than an extramarital affair."

"Then we need to search the stables. Whatever Bellini's hiding there might release Georgia from his grip and help Alfie."

Elizabeth nodded, reaching for the ignition. "We'll need a torch."

The headlamps flickered on, illuminating a cluttered workbench and shelving.

Meli pointed, exiting the motorcar. "There."

Elizabeth killed the engine as her cousin retrieved the torch. Its beam cut through the darkness.

"Ready?"

They exited the garage, the gravel drive crunching beneath their feet as they made their way to the stables, their senses alert.

"We need to be vigilant. Bellini's men could be hanging about."

The stables materialised from the darkness, a foreboding presence against the night sky. Elizabeth hesitated at the threshold.

A horse snorted softly in the shadows. "Where do we start?" Meli breathed.

"Let's start with Tommy's office."

Elizabeth swept her torch beam across the stable interior, the horses shifting restlessly at their approach. At the far end, a simple door marked the trainer's domain.

Keeping the beam low, Elizabeth tried the handle. It turned easily, granting them access to the small space beyond.

She directed the torch inside, revealing the cramped room. Saddles and bridles hung from pegs on one wall, while a cluttered desk dominated the other. Stacks of papers and training schedules teetered precariously atop it.

"What are we looking for?"

"Anything suspicious."

Meli opened a cupboard and held up a small glass of vial. "What about morphine?"

Elizabeth glanced inside, noting half a dozen vials. "That's probably normal for a stable of this size."

Meli stumbled in the gloom, her foot catching on a feed sack. The impact elicited a muffled clink of glass.

"That doesn't sound like grains to me." Elizabeth handed Meli the torch before tearing open the top of the sack. Beneath the layer of grain, her fingers brushed against something unexpected – smooth, cool glass nestled in cloth.

She unwrapped it carefully, revealing a vial identical to those in the cupboard. Elizabeth repeated the action several times, each yielding the same result.

"There must be dozens in there," Meli murmured, peering over Elizabeth's shoulder as she withdrew another vial.

Elizabeth nodded grimly. "The question is, what do we do with them?"

"I'd put them back where you found them if you know what's good for you." Tommy's gruff voice cut through the darkness, causing them both to start. "Then forget about it."

Elizabeth stiffened. She turned towards Tommy's shadowy outline. "Why, where did they come from?" Her voice was steady despite the sudden tension.

His eyes narrowed. "With all due respect, Lady Elizabeth, you'll need to take that up with Lady Fairfax and the doc. I'm just here to look after the horses, not poke my nose into things that don't concern me."

He shifted his weight, his stance uneasy. "It's not safe to be poking about the stables at night. There's all sorts who might be around." He gestured towards the door, his meaning clear. "Best you head back to the house now."

Elizabeth met Meli's gaze, a flicker of understanding passing between them. "Your're quite right, of course. Come, Meli."

Once out of sight of the stables, Elizabeth slowed her pace and partially unscrewed the torch's battery compartment until the torch's beam dimmed.

"Elizabeth, what on earth are you doing?"

"Tommy seemed very anxious to be rid of us, don't you think?"

Meli nodded.

"So I want to find out why."

They crept back towards the stables. An engine's rumble broke the silence, growing louder. But it didn't sound like a motorcar.

They watched as Tommy emerged from the stables, his torch bobbing as he made his way to the barn. Headlamps pierced the darkness as a lorry approached.

"A delivery, at this hour? What on earth?"

Elizabeth grabbed Meli's wrist and tugged, leading her towards the barn.

They squeezed through a gap in the barn's weathered boards and crouched behind a wall of hay. Outside, a flatbed lorry rumbled to a stop, its cargo of hay bales stacked high.

Headlamps and torches illuminated the darkness as workers began unloading. Meli squinted at one of the farmhands. "I recognise him ... but I can't recall from where."

A flash of metal peeked from a hay bale. Elizabeth's fingers dug into Meli's arm. "Did you see that?" she hissed.

Meli pinched her nose, suppressing a sneeze. Tommy's torch beam cut across the barn. Elizabeth froze, certain his gaze had found hers. But the light moved on, and Tommy returned to his task.

Meli's sneeze exploded in the silence.

"What was that?" one of the men barked.

Elizabeth's heart hammered as she and Meli froze.

"Just the horses," Tommy drawled, not missing a beat.

The workers turned back to their job. Elizabeth caught Meli's eye, and they slipped away into the night and back to the house.

They crept into Rosewood Park through the back door. The night's revelations churned in Elizabeth's mind as they entered the foyer. Meli's fingers suddenly gripped her elbow.

"That man with the hay bales." Meli's free hand flew to her mouth. "I've remembered where I saw him. He was at Adelina's, with Antonio."

Elizabeth turned, her gaze sharp. "You're certain?"

Meli nodded, her eyes steady. "Absolutely."

Footsteps echoed from the hallway as Pritchard appeared, his shoulders slumped and eyes heavy-lidded. He inclined his head in greeting, his voice weary as he addressed them. "Good evening, Lady Elizabeth, Miss Diomaros. Did you have a pleasant evening?"

Elizabeth and Meli exchanged a glance before Elizabeth replied. "It was certainly ... eventful." She paused, her tone shifting. "How is Lord Fairfax faring? Has his condition improved?"

Pritchard's expression darkened. "I'm afraid not, my lady. Lady Fairfax has been at his bedside all evening."

"Has the doctor been summoned?"

"Not yet, my lady. Lady Fairfax believes it to be a severe case of influenza and is monitoring the situation."

Elizabeth inhaled sharply. "Please keep me informed, and do let Lady Fairfax know I'm available to sit with Lord Fairfax should she need rest."

"Certainly, my lady. Can I bring you anything? A light supper, perhaps?"

"No, thank you, Pritchard."

They climbed the stairs in silence, the weight of the evening's discoveries compounded by this new worry. At the top, Meli turned to Elizabeth, her voice low. "What if it's more than just influenza?"

Elizabeth met her cousin's gaze, her expression grave. "Let's hope it isn't."

Elizabeth closed the bedroom door, her shoulders sagging as she caught sight of her bed. She placed her clutch on the vanity and sank onto the stool, studying her reflection. Her hand flew to her shoulder, patting frantically.

She leapt up, upending her clutch onto the mattress. Coins and lipstick scattered across the bedcover. No pin. She whirled to face Meli, her chest tightening. "My silver pin. It's gone."

"Are you certain?"

"Yes … I must have lost it." Elizabeth began to pace, her steps quick and uneven as she mentally retraced her steps.

Meli's voice was gentle. "Perhaps it fell off in the motorcar or at the stables."

Elizabeth halted, her eyes widening. "But what if I didn't? What if I lost it at Adelina's? Or in Enzo's office … Or in that room where Jonathan and I hid?"

Meli guided her cousin to the bed, her arm around Elizabeth's shoulders. "First thing tomorrow, we'll search Iggy's car. I'm sure it will turn up."

"But what if it doesn't? What if Bellini finds it…" Elizabeth's voice quavered. "He'll know someone's been in his inner sanctum and is on to him."

What if she'd jeopardised everything? Jonathan's investigation? The chance to free Georgia and possibly countless others from Bellini's grip. Alfie?

How could she have been so careless?

Chapter Twenty-Two

ELIZABETH STARED AT THE ceiling, her mind refusing to quiet. Sleep had eluded her, replaced by a relentless parade of questions and worries. The events at Adelina's replayed in her thoughts – the hidden room, Bellini's conversation, Jonathan's warnings. She shifted, unable to find comfort as her mind jumped to the stables, the morphine vials nestled in feed sacks, and the late-night delivery of hay bales.

But it was the loss of her silver pin that truly gnawed at her. Its absence was a constant reminder of her carelessness and the potential consequences it wreaked – had it fallen in Bellini's office, or worse, that hidden room? If discovered, it would alert Bellini that someone had been snooping around his inner sanctum, jeopardising Jonathan's investigation and her chance of clearing Alfie of involvement in the Thornton attack.

She had to find that pin.

Elizabeth rose from the bed, the chill of the room raising goosebumps on her skin. She dressed quickly, her movements practiced and silent. Meli slumbered on, oblivious, as Elizabeth slipped out of the room.

The house was still as Elizabeth made her way downstairs. She paused at the front door, listening for any sign of movement before making her way across the gravel path towards the garage.

Once inside, she began her search of Iggy's motorcar, methodically examining every inch of the interior. Her fingers traced the leather upholstery seams, probed under the floor mats, and explored the space beneath the steering column. But the silver pin remained frustratingly absent.

Elizabeth's attention shifted to Georgia's Vauxhall parked next to the Aston Martin. The memory of the previous night flashed in her mind – the strip of familiar fabric peeking from the spare wheel cover.

Perhaps Meli had been right about it being a flag or bunting, but she had to be certain. Elizabeth glanced around the empty garage, then unclipped the spare wheel cover. As she lifted it away, a bundle of cloth tumbled onto the concrete floor.

She snatched it up and examined it closely. It was indeed a set of riding silks, identical to Alfie's. Georgia's perfume clung to the fabric, and a telltale smudge of makeup stained the collar. She hastily replaced the wheel cover and silk, her mind racing with implications. Was this Alfie's silk, or had Georgia commissioned an identical set? She needed answers.

She slipped out of the garage, a distant whinny breaking the silence as she darted across the yard. A handful of bleary-eyed stable hands shuffled about, starting their morning routines. She kept to the shadows, slipping past unnoticed, and reached the narrow staircase leading to Alfie's quarters.

At Alfie's quarters, she turned the handle of the weather-beaten door. It swung open with a muted protest. She paused on the threshold, taking in the sparse room. A narrow bed, its thin blanket askew, hugged one wall. Across from it, a battered chest of drawers, its paint chipped and worn. Dim light struggled through a grimy window, barely revealing a crumpled set of riding silks on the floor.

Her mind raced back to William's tale of Georgia's daring deception years ago, riding in her brother's place. Had that been Georgia's plan, to take Alfie's place in the Grand National? If so, why hadn't Alfie told her? And what had stopped Georgia from following through?

The memory of race day surfaced – the heated exchange she'd witnessed between Alfie and Reggie, ending in Alfie's furious departure. But now, doubt crept in.

Was it really Alfie she'd seen arguing with Reggie?

After closing the door behind her, she crept down the steps and out of the stables, her eyes darting across the courtyard. As she passed the barn, her mind wandered to the previous night's peculiar hay delivery. The late hour, the unnecessary addition to an already full barn, and that curious glint she'd spotted in the torchlight – it all reeked of suspicion.

Meli's words about the supposed farm worker's connection to Antonio nagged at Elizabeth. It couldn't be a mere coincidence.

She paused, glancing back at the house. The sensible thing would be to return and inform the police. But despite the risk, Elizabeth felt an irresistible pull towards the barn. Her feet seemed to move of their own accord, carrying her closer, the need for answers outweighing her caution.

Elizabeth crept into the barn, her eyes quickly finding the fresh hay bales she'd seen delivered the night before. Their crisp edges stood out among the older, settled stacks.

She grabbed a nearby pitchfork and thrust its prongs into one of the new bales. A sharp clang echoed as metal struck metal.

She thrust her hand into the bale, and her fingers closed around something cold and heavy. A gun.

The crunch of gravel outside snapped her attention to the barn door. Someone was coming.

Elizabeth returned the weapon to its hiding place as a 'stable worker' appeared. She recognised him instantly – the very man Meli had identified last night.

His eyes narrowed as he approached. "Looking for something, miss?"

Elizabeth's mind whirred. "I lost a brooch yesterday. Thought I might have dropped it here."

The lie sounded flimsy, even to her own ears.

He crossed his arms. "Best not to linger in here alone, miss. These hay bales can be dangerous if they topple."

His words hung in the air, laced with unspoken menace.

"Of course," Elizabeth replied, forcing a smile. "Thank you for the warning."

The man stood watching as if rooted to the spot.

"I suppose I'd better be on my way."

He nodded, his gaze boring into her back as she walked away.

Elizabeth hurried from the barn to the house, her thoughts running through the implications. What could have driven Georgia to align herself with someone as dangerous as Bellini? Surely she comprehended the risks someone like him posed. Unless ... the leverage he held over her was so serious that compliance was her only option.

She shuddered as she considered the far-reaching consequences of Bellini's operations. His influence extended well beyond these stables, leaving a trail of ruined lives in its wake. Those hidden caches of drugs and weapons promised nothing but misery and violence.

Elizabeth paused at the side door, the full weight of her discovery sinking in. This wasn't just about Georgia anymore. Bellini's operation at Rosewood threatened countless lives.

She had to act now. The police needed to see this evidence firsthand.

"Aintree Police Station, please," she said as soon as the operator answered.

Moments later, the line clicked.

"Aintree Police Station, Constable Parker speaking."

"This is Lady Elizabeth Hawthorne. I need to speak with Chief Inspector Wainwright immediately. It's urgent."

"One moment, Lady Elizabeth." The silence stretched interminably. "I'm afraid the Chief Inspector is unavailable, my lady. He'll return your call when he can."

Elizabeth's grip tightened on the receiver. "You don't understand. This is a matter of utmost urgency–"

"I'll inform him, my lady." The line went dead.

Elizabeth tapped her fingers against the side table, willing the constable to return. Finally, he did.

"I'm sorry, my lady. The Chief Inspector is still unavailable and he'll contact you when he has time."

"Very well. Thank you, Constable." She replaced the receiver. Wainwright's refusal to listen, while predictable, still rankled. Her thoughts turned to Jonathan. If only she had some way to contact him.

Worry gnawed at her as memories of Adelina's flooded back. Jonathan could look after himself, but against Bellini and Sabini together? She shook her head as if trying to remove the scenarios playing out in her mind as she swept through the foyer, her frustration evident in the set of her shoulders. Mrs Langley emerged from the hallway, tea tray in hand.

"Good morning, Mrs Langley." She forced a smile, momentarily pushing her concerns aside. "Is that for Lady Fairfax?"

Mrs Langley nodded, her expression weary. "Yes, my lady. She's been sitting with Lord Fairfax all night. He's not at all well."

Elizabeth hesitated, concern for Iggy warring with the need to speak with Georgia. "I could take that up if you'd like. Perhaps I might convince Lady Fairfax to rest for a while."

Mrs Langley's shoulders sagged. "Oh, would you, my lady? I've tried, but Lady Fairfax is quite determined to stay by his side."

Elizabeth accepted the tray, her fingers tightening on the handles. The timing was far from ideal, and she hated to press Georgia for answers while Iggy was ill, but the riding silk could be crucial to unravelling this mystery. With Bellini's reach proving far more extensive than she'd imagined, she couldn't afford to leave any stone unturned.

Outside Iggy's room, Elizabeth paused, the weight of the tray suddenly heavy in her hands.

She'd have to tread carefully, balancing her genuine concern for her friends with her need for answers. The riding silk, Bellini's reach, Georgia's secrecy – how did it all connect?

Chapter Twenty-Three

Elizabeth nudged open the heavy oak door to Iggy's bedroom, the tea tray balanced precariously in her hands. As she stepped inside, the air pressed against her – dense, stagnant, and uncomfortably warm. It clung to her skin and filled her lungs, the crisp promise of spring withering at the threshold.

Heavy velvet curtains sagged from their rails, permitting only the thinnest rays of morning light to infiltrate the room. These slivers of brightness only served to emphasise the room's oppressive gloom, cutting through dust motes that swirled lazily in the stagnant air.

In the hearth, embers smouldered, occasionally flaring with a weak, orange pulse. The fire's feeble light scarcely reached the dark wood panelling, leaving the room's corners veiled in shadows.

As her eyes adjusted to the dimness, the room's details emerged from the gloom like a developing photograph. The imposing four-poster bed dominated the space, its heavy burgundy curtains drawn back to reveal the pale figure lying motionless beneath the covers.

Elizabeth's gaze swept across the room, finally settling on a figure by the bedside. Georgia sat there, her hand gently moving along Iggy's arm. As Elizabeth drew closer, Georgia's whisper reached her ears.

"...not long now, my love." The words, soft as a breath, sent a chill through Elizabeth.

"Georgia?" Elizabeth approached the bed, tea tray in hand.

Georgia turned, her face a mask of exhaustion. Gone was the spirited, larger-than-life personality that usually filled any room she occupied. She regarded Elizabeth with a weary expression, all traces of her usual vivacity absent.

"I've brought some tea." Elizabeth set the tray on a nearby table. "Perhaps after we've had a cup, you could rest for a bit? I'd be happy to sit with Iggy."

Georgia's eyes, usually bright, now dull and unfocused, met Elizabeth's. "No." Her voice came out hoarse. "I have to be here."

"Have you called for the doctor?"

Georgia shook her head, a jerky, almost mechanical movement.

"Shall I telephone him or summon Pritchard?"

Georgia shook her head. "No … it's better this way."

Elizabeth's unease grew as she studied Georgia's face. The flickering firelight accentuated the sharp angles of her cheekbones. This was not the Georgia she knew. This was a stranger wearing her friend's face.

Georgia turned to the tea tray. "Elizabeth, honey, fetch a blanket from the wardrobe, would you? I think Iggy's a little cold. I'll pour the tea."

Elizabeth hesitated, the fire's warmth prickling her skin. "Of course." She rose and retrieved a thin coverlet, draping it over Iggy before settling into one of the chairs. She picked up her cup, inhaling the fragrant steam before sipping her tea. The room was quiet save for the crackle of the fire. She watched as Georgia's gaze rested on Iggy.

"I wish you'd seen him back in the day, Elizabeth. The moment I first laid eyes on him, it was like the whole world just … stopped. He was standing there, so tall and handsome … every inch the dashing explorer." A girlish smile spread across Georgia's face. "I knew right then I was going to marry him."

Georgia shook her head, a soft sigh escaping her. "Iggy took some convincing. He fretted about the age gap, and my parents weren't thrilled either. But once I set my mind to something … Well, we were married six weeks later."

Elizabeth listened as she sipped her tea, Georgia's words painting a vivid picture of their whirlwind romance.

The fire popped.

Iggy stirred, his eyelids fluttering. "Thirsty," he mumbled.

Georgia immediately moved to his side. "Here you go, my love." She gently held the cup to his lips, allowing him to take a small sip.

Elizabeth set her cup down. "Georgia, I really think we ought to call for the doctor."

"No," she snapped. "He's my husband. I can take care of him."

Elizabeth stifled a yawn, blinking slowly. The lack of sleep from the previous night was catching up with her, amplified by the room's oppressive warmth.

Georgia's voice softened as she continued, "Did you know Iggy was part of Shackleton's Discovery Expedition?"

She nodded, her eyelids heavy as Georgia recanted the tale of Iggy's adventures in Antarctica and how it cost him two toes. "Don't let your tea get cold, honey."

Elizabeth straightened in her seat, trying to shake off the fatigue.

"Do you know we'd planned to go to Kenya?" Her eyes sparkled briefly with the memory, then dimmed. "Before the accident."

The shift in Georgia's demeanour was palpable. Her shoulders sagged, and bitterness crept into her voice. "I thought … I was so sure he'd bounce back quickly. Iggy was always so strong, so vital, nothing ever kept him down for long."

She shook her head, a rueful smile playing on her lips. "I dismissed the doctor's words when they warned me about his age affecting his recovery. Iggy? Old? It seemed absurd."

Georgia's gaze drifted to Iggy's still form. "But they were right. After he pulled through the worst of it, everything slowed to a crawl. Now look at him." Her voice cracked slightly. "He's become just another boring, middle-aged man."

As if on cue, Iggy stirred again. Georgia rose swiftly, moving to his side. "Here, darling, have some more tea." She gently tilted his head forward, bringing the cup to his lips. Elizabeth noticed Iggy's breaths growing shallower as he sipped.

Georgia coaxed him to take another small sip, her earlier bitterness masked by tender concern. "There you go, my love. That's better, isn't it?"

Elizabeth's head felt heavy, her thoughts growing sluggish. She blinked slowly, trying to clear the fog that seemed to be settling over her thoughts. "Georgia," she began, struggling to find the right words. "About Reggie ... I hope you don't mind me asking, but ... I've heard he was quite the charmer with the ladies and–"

"Me and Reggie?" Georgia's laugh was sharp, brittle. "Reggie? That spineless, pathetic excuse for a man?" She shook her head, disgust twisting her features.

Elizabeth's vision swam, her thoughts slipping away like water through her fingers. She squinted at Georgia, trying to focus. "Enzo Bellini," she mumbled, the name feeling thick on her tongue. "You and him ... how ...?" She trailed off, unable to complete the thought.

"It's Reggie Black's fault that I got mixed up with Bellini in the first place..." Georgia sighed heavily. "Oh what the heck ... you won't remember this when you wake up anyway. Reggie offered to take care of Iggy if I paid off his gambling debts to Bellini," she said, her voice low and bitter. "But once I'd settled up, he backpedalled. Claimed he wasn't serious." She laughed, a harsh, ugly sound. "So I had to take care of him before he went to the police. I didn't know he'd already blabbed to Bellini."

"You tried to have Iggy killed?" Elizabeth's eyes widened, her heart pounding as she struggled to process Georgia's words. "But why … I thought you loved Iggy."

"I do love him … that's why I did it." Georgia jumped to her feet and began pacing. "Do you think Iggy wants to spend the rest of his life like this?" She spun to face Elizabeth. "Do you think he enjoys being an invalid … trapped in this half-life? I'm saving him."

Elizabeth's mind reeled, horror piercing through the fog clouding her thoughts. Georgia's confession echoed in her ears – Reggie's murder, Iggy's attempted murder.

Georgia watched Elizabeth, a hint of satisfaction glinting in her eyes. Elizabeth fought against the heaviness in her limbs, her vision blurring. As she struggled to focus, her gaze drifted to Iggy's bedside table. A glass vial caught her eye, and suddenly, the pieces clicked into place. The tea. Georgia had laced it with morphine.

Elizabeth's gaze darted between the cup in Georgia's hand and Iggy's face. Her body felt like lead, but adrenaline surged through her veins. She lurched forward, knocking the cup from

Georgia's grasp. It hit the floor with a sharp crack, tea seeping into the rug.

Georgia's eyes flashed dangerously. In one swift motion, she whipped a syringe from beneath a folded napkin on the bedside table, its needle glinting menacingly in the fire light.

Georgia lunged, syringe in hand. Elizabeth twisted, barely deflecting the attack. They crashed into each other, stumbling backwards. Elizabeth's fingers clamped around Georgia's wrists, straining to keep the needle at bay. The syringe trembled between them, its tip a hair's breadth from Elizabeth's throat.

Elizabeth's strength waned as she grappled with Georgia. They lurched across the room, locked in a frenzied tussle. Elizabeth's foot caught on the rug, throwing them off balance. They careened into a side table, upending it, porcelain shards skittering across the wooden floorboards.

Georgia's face hovered inches from Elizabeth's, her eyes blazing with manic determination. The room spun around Elizabeth, her vision blurring as the morphine coursed through her veins. The needle crept closer. Elizabeth's fingers, slick with sweat, slipped on Georgia's wrists.

Elizabeth twisted, her elbow connecting with Georgia's ribs. She grunted, her grip loosening for a split second. Elizabeth wrenched free and staggered away. But her legs betrayed her, buckling beneath her weight. She fell hard, her palms stinging as porcelain shards dug in.

Georgia advanced, syringe in hand. Elizabeth scrambled backwards, porcelain shards slicing her palms. Her limbs felt leaden, her vision narrowing to a pinpoint.

She collapsed onto her back, chest heaving. Georgia knelt over her, face twisted. The syringe glinted as she raised it, needle poised above Elizabeth's neck.

Elizabeth's eyelids fluttered, darkness encroaching. The door exploded inwards, hinges shrieking. A whirlwind of motion culminated in a sickening thud.

Georgia crumpled.

Elizabeth's vision blurred and faded, leaving only the hazy image of Meli wielding a dented tea tray.

Chapter Twenty-Four

THE LIVERPOOL-BOUND TRAIN STOOD poised at Aintree station, steam billowing from its engine in great plumes. Elizabeth sank into the plush velvet seat of the first-class compartment, her fingers resting on the newspaper in her lap. The bold type of the headline proclaimed, *YOUNG JOCKEY ALFIE TANNER VINDICATED, DECLARED RIGHTFUL WINNER OF GRAND NATIONAL.*

Beneath it, a smaller headline caught her eye: "Champion Jockey Reggie Black's Tragic Demise Shocks Racing World". She'd not only witnessed these events but had been thrust into their very heart.

She watched the flurry of activity on the platform, her thoughts miles away at Hawthorne

Hall. Tomorrow's gathering offered a welcome diversion from recent events. Alfie's homecoming, vindicated and victorious, was cause for celebration, indeed.

Her gaze drifted back to the article detailing Reggie Black's demise. The newspaper spun a tale of a champion jockey's tragic downfall, claiming an opiate addiction had led to a fatal overdose and his deadly fall. She knew the truth that lay behind those carefully crafted words – there had been no addiction, no accidental overdose.

Reggie's death was the result of Georgia's desperation. Elizabeth shuddered, recalling the wild look in Georgia's eyes that day in Iggy's bedroom, the disconnect between her actions and reality. How had her friend's mind become so warped, so detached from the consequences of her choices?

Across from her, Meli shifted restlessly, her gaze darting between the window and her cousin. The usual sparkle in her eyes had dimmed, replaced by a weariness that seemed out of place on her young face.

"I can't believe how much has happened since we arrived in Aintree." Meli glanced at the compartment door before continuing. "And to think that Georgia … tried to murder Iggy. And you."

Elizabeth folded the newspaper and set it aside. "If it wasn't for your quick thinking with that tea tray, things might have ended very differently."

"Don't." Meli winced, her eyes squeezing shut. "If I'd arrived even a few moments later…" She exhaled sharply, then looked directly at Elizabeth. "What will happen to Georgia now?"

Elizabeth sighed, her gaze drifting to the bustling platform outside the window. "According to William, she's not well enough to stand trial. She'll likely remain at Broadmoor Asylum for the criminally insane."

"Do you think she'll ever … recover?" Meli asked.

"It's unlikely." Elizabeth looked away." Caroline told me that when she visited, Georgia was 'waiting' for Iggy," Elizabeth added. "She was convinced he was coming to pick her up for an adventure to Kenya. Something about joining a safari expedition in the Masai Mara."

"She doesn't remember any of it? Not even…" Meli's voice trailed off, unable to voice the horrific act.

"No." Elizabeth clasped her hands tightly in her lap. "According to the doctors, Georgia's mind has retreated to a time before Iggy's accident. For her, these past two years simply don't exist."

"What about that set of racing silks you found hidden in Georgia's spare wheel cover?" Meli asked. "Do you think she wore it in order to frame Alfie for Reggie's murder?"

Elizabeth sighed, shaking her head. "I've wondered about that too. With Georgia's current state, I doubt we'll ever know for certain. Her motives, her plans … they're all locked away in a part of her mind we can't reach."

"To think how close she came to ruining Alfie's life," Meli mused. "I just can't fathom it. Georgia had everything – beauty, money, a husband who adored her." Her tone softened. "How was Iggy this morning? Any improvement?"

Elizabeth shook her head, her expression grim. "I'm afraid not. If anything, he seemed more withdrawn. The doctors say he's still in shock."

"Do you think he'll return to Rosewood once he's released?"

Elizabeth shook her head. "No. He's going to stay with his old friend Percy Fawcett in Devon. His doctor thinks the change of scenery will do him good."

Meli leaned forward in her seat, her brow creasing as she peered close. "Isn't that your Mr Ashcroft?"

Elizabeth's gaze snapped to the platform. "He's hardly my Mr Ashcroft, Meli." She rolled her eyes at her cousin's teasing, but there was no denying the quickening of her pulse as unbidden memories surfaced. Waking after Georgia's attack, she'd found Jonathan in her room, uncharacteristically dishevelled, his tie askew and jacket rumpled.

Meli had been relentless with her teasing later. "You should have seen him," she'd said, eyes dancing. "Prowling about like a caged tiger, pestering the doctor. He was in quite a state."

The compartment door rattled open. Jonathan ducked inside, his eyes seeking Elizabeth's. "I'm glad I caught you," he said, sinking into the seat beside Meli. He leaned forward, lowering his voice. "There've been some developments I thought you'd want to hear about."

Meli's eyebrows arched, a mischievous glint in her eye as she glanced between Elizabeth and Jonathan. Elizabeth pretended not to notice. "What sort of updates?"

Jonathan's eyes darted to the compartment door before settling back on Elizabeth. "Bellini's vanished," he said, keeping his voice low. "The car showroom, Adelina's – both emptied overnight. Not a trace left behind as if they never existed."

Elizabeth felt her breath catch. "When did this happen?"

"Sometime in the last twenty-four hours," Jonathan replied. "The police are baffled. It's as if he knew they were closing in."

"Do you think it could be the same person who ordered Wainwright to shut down his investigation into Thornton's attack?" Meli asked. "We thought it was Georgia, but it could easily have been someone else with influence, someone on Bellini's payroll."

He nodded slowly. "It's possible. Bellini has connections everywhere. He'd certainly have the means to interfere with a police investigation."

Elizabeth's fingers tightened on the edge of her seat. "Do they have any idea of his whereabouts?"

Jonathan's eyes narrowed. "The police have no solid leads. Italy's been suggested, but it's far too obvious for someone like Bellini. He's cunning, unpredictable. I suspect he's still close by, biding his time."

"What about Rosewood Park?" Elizabeth's gaze remained fixed on Jonathan. "Did the police search the barn?"

Jonathan exhaled slowly. "They did. Nothing unusual turned up. If Bellini had been using it, he'd cleared everything out well before the police arrived."

"What about Dr Franklin?" Meli asked. "Surely they must have questioned him about all the morphine we found?"

Jonathan shook his head. "Franklin bought himself a one-way ticket to Australia, left a couple of days ago."

"So that's it, Bellini's getting away scot-free?"

"With Bellini vanished and no one willing to talk, the police couldn't make anything stick."

"What about Sam Thornton?" Meli's fingers drummed against her knee. "Wasn't he laundering Bellini's money through his father's shop?"

A shadow crossed Jonathan's face. "No one's seen hide nor hair of him. There's talk his disappearance might be Bellini's doing. He doesn't take kindly to grasses who blab to the police."

Elizabeth studied his face, looking for any telltale signs. Had Jonathan deliberately exposed Sam as the grass to protect Alfie?

The train whistle blew, signalling their imminent departure.

"I should go," Jonathan said, rising. His eyes met Elizabeth's, holding her gaze a moment longer than necessary. "Lady Elizabeth, a pleasure as always." He turned to Meli. "Miss Diomaros, it's been a delight."

The train lurched forward as Jonathan stepped onto the platform. His figure shrank into the distance as the train pulled away, yet his gaze remained locked on Elizabeth.

"Well, my dear cousin." Meli's voice cut through her musings. "I think it's safe to say that Mr Ashcroft is indeed your Mr Ashcroft, cousin."

Elizabeth turned from the window, a betraying warmth creeping up her cheeks. "Honestly, Meli, you're incorrigible." She pressed her lips together, fighting a smile.

As Aintree faded from view, Elizabeth found herself pondering the conundrum that Jonathan Ashcroft presented.

He was charming yet secretive, heroic yet evasive.

A human kaleidoscope, constantly shifting.

But perhaps some mysteries just weren't meant to be solved.

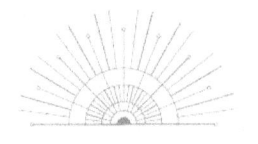

Epilogue

ELIZABETH LEANED BACK IN her chair, savouring her morning tea. Across the table, William rustled his newspaper, brow furrowed as he scanned the pages. Caroline sat beside him, her gaze distant as she swirled her tea with a silver spoon. Meli, uncharacteristically subdued, pushed the remains of her breakfast around the plate with her fork.

As she sipped her tea, her thoughts drifted to the recent celebrations at Hawthorne Hall, their family estate in Surrey, where they'd gathered to honour Alfie's Grand National victory. A warmth spread through her chest as she recalled Alfie's beaming face and his parents' obvious pride, but the memory soured as she thought of the events that had led to Alfie's wrongful arrest.

Her thoughts turned to Iggy, still recovering in Devon, and to Georgia, now a patient at Broadmoor Hospital. The doctors had diagnosed a mental derangement, confining her indefinitely.

Georgia's role in Reggie's murder and her attempt on Iggy's life had left them all reeling. But despite Georgia's heinous actions, Elizabeth found herself wrestling with an unexpected pang of sympathy. The warm-hearted woman she'd known seemed irreconcilable with the cold-blooded murderer Georgia had become.

The dining room door opened and Dalton entered, a silver tray balanced in his hands. He distributed the morning's post, setting William's letters beside his plate before placing two envelopes in front of Elizabeth.

"Your correspondence, my Lord, my Lady."

"Thank you, Dalton," William and Elizabeth murmured, their voices overlapping. Dalton nodded and quietly left the room.

Elizabeth slid her finger under the flap of the first envelope, unfolding the letter inside. As her eyes scanned the page, a small crease appeared between her brows. "Oh," she said softly, surprise colouring her voice. "I'd completely forgotten about this."

Caroline looked up from her tea. "Not bad news, I hope?"

"No, nothing like that." Elizabeth's lips curved into a small smile. "I'd forgotten about a charity auction I won months ago. The prize is a long weekend on Ingleby Island to watch Comet Aletheia."

William lowered his newspaper. "Ingleby Island? Thomas Ingleby's place?"

"I believe so. Why do you ask?"

William set his paper aside. "Ingleby's barely been seen since the scandal a couple of years ago, when his partner embezzled funds from their bank's customers and fled to South America."

"Ah, yes," Caroline nodded, recollection dawning on her face. "I remember reading about that in the newspapers. It was quite the scandal." She turned to her husband. "I wonder what prompted him to open his island. An event like Comet Aletheia is bound to attract considerable interest."

"Papa told me about a comet mentioned in some scrolls discovered at Delphi. It appears every few centuries and the ancient Greeks believed it revealed hidden truths." Meli smiled. "But Papa says it's not the comet that reveals secrets – it's the people."

William leaned back in his chair, fingers drumming lightly on the table. "Your father's insight serves him well. Human nature will reveal its true motives, regardless of any celestial event."

Meli's expression grew serious. "Do you think Ingleby Island holds any secrets of its own?"

Elizabeth's shoulders tensed slightly. "I certainly hope not. After our recent adventure in Aintree, I'm rather looking forward to some peace and tranquillity."

"I'm not surprised. Murder, Alfie's arrest, illegal gambling dens, gangsters…" Meli counted off on her fingers. "When you list it all out like that, it does sound rather overwhelming."

Meli's words hung in the air, a sobering reminder of the gravity of recent events.

Caroline glanced around the table before leaning in slightly. "What about Bellini?" she asked, her voice barely above a whisper. "Any word on his whereabouts?"

William's jaw tightened as he met Elizabeth's gaze. "I spoke with Ashcroft yesterday." He paused, his voice dropping lower. "It's as if Bellini's vanished without a trace."

Jonathan. Her breath caught, the name conjuring a whirlwind of conflicting emotions.

She met her brother's gaze, wary of revealing too much. "You spoke with Mr Ashcroft?"

"Yes, I ran into him at my club."

She paused, choosing her words with care. "Did he … mention anything else?"

"You know Ashcroft – plays his cards close to his chest. But he believes it's only a matter of time before Bellini resurfaces."

Elizabeth slid her finger under the second envelope's flap. A silver pin tumbled out with the note, its letter A glinting up at her mockingly.

Her stomach twisted as she unfolded the note.

I thought it was time I returned this to you. Until next time, Lady Elizabeth.

She swallowed hard, her mind racing.

Bellini knew what she'd done.

And now he was taunting her.

Flaunting his ability to reach her any time he wanted.

Curious about how Georgia and Iggy first met? Then join my newsletter to access this exclusive bonus scene.

https://dl.bookfunnel.com/9fy3zwamhb

If you enjoyed 'Murder at the Grand National', then check out Book 5 in the Lady Elizabeth Hawthorne Mystery series,

'Murder at the Observatory'

When a rare celestial event ends in tragedy, Lady Elizabeth Hawthorne's island retreat becomes a deadly paradise.

With the cosmic clock ticking and danger lurking in every shadow, Elizabeth must align the stars of truth before the killer strikes again. In this deadly game of celestial chess, can she outmanoeuvre a killer who seems to map the sphere with deadly precision? Or will she be eclipsed by their murderous machinations?

https://books2read.com/u/mg6x7v

Newsletter

Join my Newsletter to receive your FREE copy of Shadow of the Desert Queen, and keep up to date with all the news about new releases, giveaways, promotions, etc.
https://dl.bookfunnel.com/1x00ah4bcx

Dedication

For my crazy, funny, mad, full-on family, who drive me nuts, mostly.
But I wouldn't have it any other way.
xxx

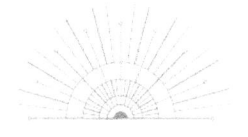

Also by Olivia Rose

MURDER ON THE SS ANDROMEDA

Champagne, caviar, and a side of murder.

When death crashes the party aboard the luxurious SS Andromeda, Lady Elizabeth Hawthorne's mission to escort a priceless Greek artifact to London takes a sinister turn. The captain's mysterious demise plunges Elizabeth into a deadly game of cat and mouse, where every passenger is a suspect and every smile could mask murderous intent.

Teaming up with lifelong alley, Major Sinclair, Elizabeth dives into a labyrinth of secrets and lies. As they navigate clandestine soirees and whispered conspiracies, the line between ally and adversary blurs. With each uncovered clue, the danger mounts, and trust becomes as fragile as crystal stemware.

Racing against time and a killer's cunning, Elizabeth and Major Sinclair must unravel the twisted web of deceit before the Andromeda docks in Liverpool. But in this floating world of glittering facades and hidden agendas, one misstep could turn their investigation deadly.

Can Elizabeth unmask the murderer lurking among the elite, or will she become the next victim in this high-stakes game of death on the high seas?

https://books2read.com/u/bpnBjX

MURDER AT MAYFIELD MANOR

Blackmail, betrayal and a body in the bath.
Lady Elizabeth Hawthorne's joyous reunion with childhood friend Clemmi Mayfield takes a

sinister turn when she uncovers a chilling web of secrets: a hidden marriage, vicious blackmail, and the Countess Magdalena von Habsfeld dead in her bath.

As a relentless blizzard seals the manor, trapping guests and their dark pasts within its frozen walls, suspicion falls on everyone – including Clemmi herself.

Once again thrust into an uneasy alliance with the enigmatic Jonathan Ashcroft, Elizabeth plunges into a labyrinth of decades-old secrets and fresh betrayals. With each revelation, the danger mounts, and she realizes that in this house of lies, even her closest friend could be a deadly enemy.

Racing against both the clock and the elements, Elizabeth must unravel the twisted threads of deceit before the killer strikes again.

But in this snow-bound manor of secrets and shadows, can Elizabeth unmask the killer before she becomes the final victim?

https://books2read.com/u/mlMzDA

MURDER ON THE FRENCH RIVIERA

Diamonds, deceit, and a deadly masquerade.

A scandalous royal murder shatters the Hawthorne family's Riviera holiday, crushing Aunt Beatrice's hopes for her cash-strapped nephew, Alexander, the Earl of Wexford, to marry the Italian princess and save his crumbling estate.

Faced with international scrutiny, the Chief Inspector hastily pins the gruesome crime on the Earl, branding him a murderous fortune hunter.

Refusing to let Alexander fall victim to the Chief Inspector's machinations, Elizabeth and her audacious cousin Meli plunge headlong into a high-stakes investigation. As they peel back the glittering veneer of Riviera society, they uncover a sinister tapestry of betrayal, blackmail, and deadly alliances. With each revelation, the danger mounts, and the cousins find themselves caught in a treacherous game where one false move could cost them everything.

With Alexander's freedom at stake and a looming scandal threatening to ruin the family's reputation, Elizabeth must unmask the true murderer before the Earl's fate is sealed forever.

But in this gilded cage of luxury and vice, can she trust anyone?

https://books2read.com/u/4A1JPp

MURDER AT THE OBSERVATORY

Galaxies, guile, and a deadly night sky.

When a rare celestial event ends in tragedy, Lady Elizabeth Hawthorne's island retreat becomes a deadly paradise. The celebrated astronomer Professor Magnus Whitaker is found dead – an apparent suicide after a humiliating failure. But the constellation of clues points to a more sinister truth.

With each guest harbouring their own dark matter, she must navigate a treacherous maze of lies and betrayal. As whispers of blackmail and long-buried secrets orbit the secluded island, the line between ally and adversary blurs like a distant nebula.

With the cosmic clock ticking and danger lurking in every shadow, Elizabeth must align the stars of truth before the killer strikes again. In this deadly game of celestial chess, can she outmanoeuvre a killer who seems to map the sphere with deadly precision? Or will she be eclipsed by their murderous machinations?

https://books2read.com/u/mg6x7v

MURDER AT THE PALACE PIER

Artists, aristocrats, and a masterclass in murder.

Swept into Brighton's dazzling world of artists' studios and bohemian nights by her free-spirited cousin Gigi, Lady Elizabeth's summer takes a dark turn when a renowned artist is found dead on the Palace Pier. Worse still, Gigi's closest friend – a celebrated model on the brink of a prestigious engagement – stands accused of his murder.

As Elizabeth delves deeper, she uncovers a masterpiece of deception spanning a decade – an illicit affair, a desperate cover-up, and a web of forgery that entangles both the criminal underworld and aristocratic society.

With suspects ranging from a vengeful rival artist to a blackmailed lord, Elizabeth must separate genuine clues from clever forgeries. Each revelation paints a darker picture, and someone is determined to keep the truth hidden behind a carefully crafted canvas of lies.

In Brighton's glittering art scene, Elizabeth must expose a killer driven to murder by an artist's brush. But with every suspect concealing their own dark canvas, will she uncover the killer's signature – or become their final masterpiece?

https://books2read.com/u/mgnXd7

MELI'S MISADVENTURES

THE MISFORTUNE OF THE MAHARANI'S TEAR

Diamonds, desire and a Maharani's curse.

When the Maharani's Tear – a priceless diamond steeped in legend and tragedy – vanishes from Wembley's Indian Pavilion, suspicion falls on a young Greek immigrant. But Meli knows better.

Reunited with Dimitri, a friend from her own misadventure aboard the SS Andromeda, she's convinced his friend is innocent. With her faithful companion Winston at her side, Meli delves into a world of Indian princes, arranged marriages, and ancient curses.

As she navigates the dazzling displays and shadowy corners of the Exhibition, she begins to suspect the truth behind the theft is far more complex than Scotland Yard believes.

With royal tempers flaring and the threat of false justice looming, can Meli uncover the truth before an innocent man becomes the latest victim of the Maharani's curse?

https://books2read.com/u/3kgazR

About the Author

Born and raised in Wales, Olivia and her husband relocated to the Mediterranean island of Cyprus twenty years ago with their two children.

Sharing their home with five cats, two dogs, and a small colony of indigenous creepy crawlies means life is never dull.

Olivia's new series, Lady Elizabeth Hawthorne Mysteries, transports readers back in time to the vibrant and sophisticated world of 1920s England through the captivating tales of Lady Elizabeth Hawthorne. The daughter of an English lord and a Grecian adventuress, Elizabeth's lineage is as rich as the mysteries she uncovers. Her innate passion for archaeology, a legacy from her parents, propels her into a realm filled with ancient secrets and high-society intrigue.

Printed in Great Britain
by Amazon